Seriously Tasty Recipes for Sweet and Savory Pies

JENELL PARSONS

appetite
by RANDOM HOUSE

YOU WANNA PIECE OF ME?

I could have a whole chapter on dedications.
You really cannot start a business alone, and, along the way, the support that I have received from family, friends, and each and every one of you who has bought my pies has been more than I could ever have dreamed of. Trying to keep this short and sweet is a challenge for me. But overall, I dedicate this book to my mom. Almost every day since I started The Pie Hole I have called her, and I have boasted or cried with every windfall and struggle. She has listened patiently as I go on and on, she has lifted me when I thought I couldn't continue, and she has cheered me on when I have succeeded. Thank you, Mom.

Appetite by Random House® and colophon are registered trademarks of
Penguin Random House LLC.

Library and Archives Canada Cataloguing in Publication is available upon request.
ISBN: 978-0-525-61083-0
eBook ISBN: 978-0-525-61084-7

Photography by Janis Nicolay
Book and jacket design by Kelly Hill
Printed and bound in China

Published in Canada by Appetite by Random House®,
a division of Penguin Random House Canada Limited.

www.penguinrandomhouse.ca

10 9 8 7 6 5 4 3 2 1

appetite
by RANDOM HOUSE

Penguin
Random House
Canada

Contents

As soon as I found out I was writing a book, I knew "any way you slice it!" would be the opening line. When I started this crazy adventure—turning my hobby and passion for baking into The Pie Hole business—I dreamed I would write a book. Now it's happening, though, it's really scary for me to write: this book is a culmination of my passions and my very being, not just my recipes, and that's daunting. And does anyone really care how a girl from a small town moved to the big city and opened a pie shop?

Any Way You Slice It!

I remember so vividly selling my first pie, on May 29, 2011, almost a decade ago. I am a self-taught baker, and I've always just baked what I like to eat: pies. I knew that *I* loved my pies, as did my friends and family, but would other people? Friends of mine owned a hip restaurant in East Vancouver, and also held an annual Show & Shine vintage car show. With much encouragement they convinced me to set up a table full of my pies to sell at the show. I decided to channel my inner 50s housewife persona, wearing a pair of heels, a skirt, a pearl necklace, and a perfectly pressed apron. I was feeling terribly shy, and being in costume meant I could play a character and also fit in with the vintage vibe of the show. Soon, two girls approached my table in full pinup girl attire—rosy red lips and perfectly coiled hair—my first customers. I proudly walked them through my menu.

It was pretty heavy on booze-laden pies, with offerings like Bourbon Pecan Pie, Apple Jack (apples soaked in Jack Daniels), and rum-spiked Blue Hawaiian Pie, as well as my Maple French Toast Bacon Pie (page 199). The girls were intrigued by the idea of sweet maple and salty bacon together, so they bought a small Maple French Toast Bacon Pie to share. My very first sale! It was the first pie they bought that day, but it wasn't the last. I might be making this up, but I bet they had to loosen their corsets as the day went on! And it was the same with other customers, too. Throughout the day, people kept coming back for more and more pie, the remnants of flaky pie crust still on their faces and clothes as they ordered more. The feeling I felt that day—that other people loved my pie too—was validating and exhilarating! And I still feel it today.

So The Pie Hole started that afternoon at the Show & Shine car show. After that, I not only wanted, but *needed* to keep baking pies. I started borrowing friends' restaurants after hours, hauling ingredients into their kitchens, baking all night, then cleaning everything up and making sure I was out of there before they opened. Exhausted, I would set off with a car full of fresh-baked pies to farmers' markets the next morning. With my homemade chalk signs, antique apple crates, and checkered tablecloths, I set up my booth and, more often than not, would sell out of pie before the market ended. Soon I moved to work out of a friend's motorcycle warehouse, where a small, unused kitchen was offered to me in the back. In the early days my sister would come to help me. One night we peeled literally hundreds of pounds of fresh Okanagan peaches, on makeshift tables precariously squeezed in around vintage Nortons and Triumphs. I'm pretty sure she never peeled another peach after that! Eventually, I moved into a commissary kitchen, sharing the space with a bunch of other entrepreneurs, many of whom owned food trucks—and that commissary community was invaluable. Now that I was paying rent, the hustle was real—and pies needed to move out the door!

At first it was just an industrial door, with no sign. There was nothing indicating that I was in there, nothing to tell you about the pies that were being made inside. So the fact that people sought me out to buy my pies still blows my mind! (Almost as much as the fact I was able to produce hundreds of pies a week in just 64 square feet!) For a while I was content working in this space, growing my pie business at a speed I was comfortable with, coercing friends to come help me by offering wine and fun music. But bribes only work for a little while, and to preserve my friendships, I decided it was time to get serious. I stopped counting how many pies I needed to sell to make rent, and instead started hiring people to work with me to meet the demand. At one point in the tiny commissary space, I had four employees, plus me, all huddled around a five-foot stainless-steel table baking pies as fast as we could for our customers, restaurants, grocers, and butcher shops.

A few years went by and I found out that I was pregnant. Let me tell you, it was a very long, hot summer that year, making pies and cooking fillings with a growing belly! I left just five days before my little girl was born and was back after four weeks, with Cali by my side every day. I would bundle her to my chest in a baby wrap as I peeled apples, rolled dough, and baked pies. At times, she slept in a banana box cushioned with tea towels under the table, and other times I made deliveries with the car seat over one arm and a stack of pies in the other. I was determined to create something special out of the business, more than ever once I had her—not only to make her proud of me, but also to teach her a strong work ethic. Cali's very first delivery with me was a top-secret order for an unnamed celebrity. With a perfectly made pie in one arm and my newborn in another, I made my way to a fancy downtown hotel. An assistant answered the door and as I passed over the pie. I asked who it was for, just out of curiosity, and it turns out the "Governator" just loves banana cream pie!

The Pie Hole could only grow so much in that tiny commissary space, so I knew that a big business change had to happen. In February 2017, I leased a storefront in East Vancouver, and my husband, Marlon, and I jumped right into building my dream shop. Marlon put in new counters, built all the tables in the retro Formica style I loved, and hand-cut, painted, and installed over 2,000 wood tiles to create the feature wall that is now a major part of The Pie Hole's look and brand. Together we worked, with Cali crawling around in the sawdust, as fast as possible to get the space ready, and just over a month later, it was.

The day we opened we had "oven issues" (or that's what I decided to call it). Instead of flipping the "closed" sign on the door around to "open," I panicked and sent one of my new staff outside to explain that we would not be opening as planned, blaming those oven issues. A wave of disappointment swept down the lineup of people eagerly waiting outside. In reality, of course, the oven was fine; it was me who wasn't. I was terrified all over again that I wasn't ready, that for some reason the pies I'd been making for the past six years weren't good enough. But then the first person in line spotted the display case inside, full of pies. They insisted on buying a pie from it—it didn't matter if the oven was "broken"; these pies were ready to be eaten! Well, once the door opened, they all came flooding in. Despite my best efforts to remain closed that first day, we sold out of pie. It was a sellout opening day, and I never even flipped the sign on the door!

A short, crazy six months later, we outgrew our space. We were making pies as fast as we could but still turning customers away. Not only were we a regular spot for the locals, we had become a destination for people visiting Vancouver. Over the years, we've had customers from all over Canada, the US, New Zealand, and Germany (to name just a few), who all make a stop at The Pie Hole part of their Vancouver itinerary. If word was going to keep spreading, I had to be strategic about my second location and make sure it was big enough to be used as a central bakery from where we could distribute to our wholesale partners, and of course our current shop, and future shops to come.

So The Pie Hole has been a success story! When I sat down to write this cookbook, I got a bit stuck. I packed up my laptop and went to a café to write. But it wasn't just any café; it was mine (goosebumps). Sitting there with a cup of tea, I interacted with all my fellow pie lovers—from our daily regulars to those visiting for the first time. When I said I needed inspiration—well, there was certainly no shortage of it there. Our customers are

not shy (which I love!); they often approach me and share their stories every day. Stories about baking pies with their moms; about their grandmothers who carefully planned family dinners to include everyone's favorite pie; tales about the time they attempted and failed to make a pie, usually muttering about how difficult pie crust is to make. Many of their stories make me smile; some make me tear up and hug them in a warm embrace.

Recently an older woman told me that she used to come every week to The Pie Hole for apple pie with her husband. Apple pie was his favorite, and after more than 50 years of marriage, she was so happy to have found a place where he loved the pie so much that she didn't have to make it anymore! She told me that he recently passed away, but that when she's really missing him, she comes to the shop and orders a slice of apple pie, just as they did on their weekly dates.

People often open their hearts to me, sharing some of their fondest memories and real vulnerabilities with me. They walk away not knowing how their stories affect me—and they do, deeply. As I am writing this book, I keep changing the words on the page in a direct reflection of these inter-actions. Day after day, as I watch customers come through the doors, I am constantly reminded how special this thing I have created is. Over the years, countless customers have brought Pie Hole pies to their family dinners and special occasions. It's amazing and it's humbling. We have become a part of their traditions and helped contribute to their lasting memories. For me, there is nothing more special than that.

I am delighted to write this book, and to share my recipes with all of you. My hope is that you will create a little of the same magic we have at The Pie Hole in your own home.

efore I started down this path of The Pie Hole, I was an artist. I still am an artist now, I guess, but with a much more delicious medium! With painting, I believe that it doesn't matter how much money you spend on paint and brushes, the work will only be as good as the artist. I feel the same way about the art of making pies. There are a lot of tools available to you, but many of them are gimmicky and quite frankly unnecessary. Trust me, I have bought and tried them all, and in the end you just have a very cluttered "junk" drawer in your kitchen! There are, however, some tools that *are* necessary, and those are the ones I'm telling you more about here.

Tools for Making Pies

Rolling pin

A rolling pin is one of the most important tools for pie making, and I have tried pretty much every type of rolling pin you can imagine, and maybe some you can't. I held up an old glass rolling pin in an antique shop once, and the shopkeeper announced that he would be rich if he had a nickel for every person who asked what the heck this was and bet me $5 I didn't know. Of course, he didn't realize he was asking the antique-loving owner of a pie company. I explained that it was an old rolling pin designed to be filled with water and frozen to keep the pastry nice and chilled while rolling, and then used my winnings toward the purchase of that rolling pin. But, while the idea of an ice-cold rolling pin seems good, I've found that the condensation that comes with it is not great, and that's probably why this design is no longer produced.

I've used all sorts of rolling pins over the years: heavy old wooden pins with worn rustic painted handles, delicate antique milk glass pins, colorful nonstick silicone pins, and beautiful marble pins. I was even given a gorgeous hand-turned exotic wood rolling pin that was commissioned as a gift for me after I opened my first shop, but have not dared to use it as it's just that perfect.

My conclusion with rolling pins is the heavier the better. A heavy rolling pin can do a lot of the work for you, especially when you are trying to roll chilled dough. I love to use a marble pin, especially in the summer months when it's hot: not only does it have the weight of the marble helping you roll, but marble dissipates heat quickly and doesn't warm up while rolling, and that makes for happy pastry.

Pastry knife/blender

This tool has been around for as long as people have been making pies. It is used to cut the fat, whether butter, lard, or shortening, into the flour with a rocking motion when making dough. Early versions were a simple painted wooden handle with some metal wires forming a D shape. Modern versions haven't changed much: thick, rigid metal blades have replaced the wires, and the handle is usually a little more ergonomic, but the function is still very much the same. I prefer to use my own two hands when making dough though, as there is something relaxing and cathartic about rolling the butter between my fingertips and achieving that perfect texture (see page 20).

Pie weights

Using some kind of a weight is absolutely necessary when blind baking a pie crust. The goal is for the pie shell to retain its shape so it can hold the most filling possible! To prevent the sides of the pie from melting down into a little puddle, you need to line the crust and weigh it down with something. You can buy pie weights, little ceramic balls, designed for this purpose only. However, you will need multiple packs to have enough to make a single pie. Not only is this a bit of an investment, but it may end up being just another thing taking up space in your kitchen. You probably already have some suitable items in your pantry that can be used instead: things like rice, dried beans, peas, or lentils all work equally well and can be reused multiple times.

Pie plates

There are just as many varieties of pie plates as there are rolling pins. They come in so many shapes, sizes, and materials. All the recipes in this book make a standard nine-inch pie, but even in that standard size I have seen so much variation between nine-inch pie plates, so I use the word "standard" loosely! The depth, pitch of the sloped sides, and where they are measured (top or bottom) all play major factors in how much filling your pie will need. The three main materials for pie plates are metal, glass, and ceramic. Each type of pie plate has its pros and cons.

METAL Most metal pie plates are made of aluminum. The biggest pro to these plates is that they heat very quickly and can give a nice crisp crust. The downside is that they lack the aesthetic charm that you find in a beautiful ceramic pie plate. Also cutting into them to slice the pie can mark the bottom of the plate.

GLASS I really love to bake in a glass plate. Mostly because you get to lift the pie plate for a little peek-a-boo to see if the bottom has browned. They are easy to find and very inexpensive. They may not be pretty, but hey, the pie should be the star . . . am I right? I have found that you have to add about 20 percent more to the cooking time and reduce the temperature of the oven by 25°F with glass pie plates, as they take a little longer to warm up—once they get there, though, they retain a nice steady heat.

CERAMIC There are so many beautiful ceramic pie plates out there, and sometimes you can have one that has been in your family for decades. Ceramic plates have the most variation in size. People ask me all the time if they can drop off a special pie plate for us to make a pie in, and this is where I have

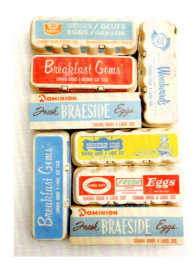

noticed the size difference the most: they are often more deep dish, which means many recipes have to be adapted (sometimes at least doubled) to fill these plates. I also find that pies baked in ceramic plates may not set as well because of all the extra filling required, and that cooking times are also often significantly longer to bake all the way through, which can put the crust in danger of burning (you will most likely need to cover the edge or even the whole top of the pie partway through to protect it from burning). I picked a beautiful deep ceramic pie plate to make one of the pies for this book. Watching the rack spin in my huge commercial oven, my heart stopped when I noticed that the plate had split in half! Pie making is not perfect; even with the thousands of pies my hands have made, mistakes still happen.

Stand mixer

If you bake regularly, you need a stand mixer. There are some beautiful ones on the market that will coordinate with any kitchen design and color, and it's definitely a solid investment for any avid home baker, not just a pie maker. Many of the recipes in this book use a stand mixer, and while sometimes you can get away with a hand mixer or basic whisk, a stand mixer will save you a great deal of time and give you results that you cannot achieve any other way.

Food processor

I use a food processor quite a bit when making pies. For pressed crusts, it is great to be able to pulse up nuts, cookies, crackers, etc. You don't need to get a huge one; just make it at least eight cups. If you are pressed for time, a food processor can be a lifesaver!

Piping bag & tips

This might seem like an odd thing to need when making a pie, but remember that not all pies have a top crust—some get decorated with whipped cream. You certainly don't have to pipe the whipped cream—you could just pile it on in what I like to call the "rustic" look—but a lot of the pies pictured in this book were decorated with a piping bag. I recommend picking up a good-quality piping bag and going a little larger than you think you need—you'll thank me when you don't have to keep refilling it! My go-to for piping tips is always the star (for making perfect rosettes), but a nice round tip for a whimsical pouf is a close second.

Measuring cups & spoons

I am an absolute sucker for a pretty set of measuring cups and spoons. There are so many cute seasonal options available, especially around Valentine's Day, Easter, and Christmas. But even though they look adorable, they are often not as reliable as a simple set of nesting spoons and cups that are easy to use, read, and clean. And you will be much less sad when you chip or break one (I am so hard on my tools).

Kitchen scale

The alternative to measuring cups and spoons is to measure ingredients by weight. As The Pie Hole has continued to grow, we need to stay very consistent, so most of my measuring spoons and cups have been packed away to make room for the scales. Let me give you two reasons why:

WEIGHING YOUR INGREDIENTS GIVES YOU MUCH MORE CONSISTENT RESULTS. Most bakers will tell you that precision is key when baking. I am a rebel and don't always follow these rules, but adding a splash of this and a sploosh of that can get you in trouble. (My team has learned my language now: "splash" equals a teaspoon and "sploosh" equals a tablespoon, but you just have to join me in the kitchen to find out what a "shimmy" is!)

DISHES. WHO REALLY LIKES DOING THOSE? Washing all the little cups and spoons after you have just slaved away making a pie? No, thank you. With a scale you can put your mixing bowl directly onto the scale and measure right into it. Just hit the tare/zero button between ingredients to zero the scale and get accurate measurements every time.

Baking sheets

Baking pies can be messy business, and there is no real way around that. You can under-fill your pie to prevent the filling bubbling over, but do you really want to serve a sad-looking sunken pie? The most enticing pie is one that is oozing over the edge, tempting you to grab a fork and dive in—after all, is a pie that's not oozing at the edges really a pie? Placing your pie dish on a baking sheet before it goes in the oven will not only catch all the drips, but provide support when you lift the pie out of the oven.

Parchment paper

Lining your baking sheet with parchment paper makes cleanup a breeze. Parchment paper is also used for lining pie crusts before adding the weights for a blind bake.

And—this one involves some baking origami skills—you can use parchment paper to form a little piping cone. A piping cone can be so helpful for decorating your pies—to drizzle caramel or chocolate ganache overtop, for example, or if you're feeling brave, to use your nicest writing to leave a sweet message.

Bench scrapers

You can find these in most cookware shops, and they are such a wonderful tool to have in the kitchen, whether pie making or just prepping some dinner. We use bench scrapers all the time in the shop. Have you ever wondered how best to clean up all the sticky dough on the counter? How about transferring all the fresh cut veggies into the pot for that chicken pot pie? Or how you will chop down the chilled butter? How you will carefully lift the perfect decorative pastry pieces you've just hand cut? The answer is simple, and now you can do all these things with ease, using your trusty bench scraper. *Call in the next 10 minutes and you will receive two for the price of one plus free shipping!* (Sorry, I had to—it was starting to feel like an infomercial.) The short of it is, I love having a bench scraper in my kitchen and use it all the time when making pie.

Mixing bowls

Depending on the type of pie you are making, you will need mixing bowls of various sizes. When picking a set of bowls for your kitchen, think about how they will function with all your cooking and baking needs. I recommend having a larger bowl for dough if you are making it by hand. This will allow you the room needed to cut the butter in and properly mix it. If you like to use a microwave to melt butter or chocolate, pick bowls that are microwave safe, and if you use a double-boiler method you will want a bowl that can safely sit over a pot of boiling water. To save space, it's a good idea to pick up a set of bowls that nest to keep them all neat, tidy, and together in the cupboard.

Whisks & spatulas

Both of these are essential items in a kitchen and come in very handy when making certain custard and cream pies. I don't have a lot of preference when it comes to whisks. I generally have a few different sizes on hand and choose a size that is appropriate to the bowl or pot that I am working with. Not too big, not too small, but just right. For spatulas, it is good to spend a little more money on one that is heat resistant. It will last longer and can be used to make recipes like caramel that get very hot. I am also partial to something called the spoonula, a spatula with a spoon-shaped end. I find that I can use it as a spatula to effectively clean the sides of a bowl, and also for scooping and filling piping bags with all that freshly whipped cream.

Cherry pitter

It's easy to go to the store and buy frozen already pitted cherries, but you should at least once make a cherry pie from scratch with farm-fresh cherries. It is a labor of love, but as you enjoy a slice with crimson-stained fingertips you will know that it was worth it. There are all sorts of cherry pitters you can buy. The one that we used for a long time, I picked up at a local grocery store. It was supposed to pit five cherries at once, but only three to five were actually pitted. You want to be certain the pit is removed by

either giving the cherry a little squeeze or poking your finger in, as finding pits in a cherry pie is, well, the pits. Now we are so lucky to have found a local farm that not only grows cherries but pits them for us too!

Kitchen thermometer

At The Pie Hole we make Italian meringue, and to do this you need a thermometer, as it's very important that the sugar reaches a certain temperature before being added to the egg whites. There are different types of thermometers available, such as a candy thermometer, which usually has a little clip on the side, to clip the thermometer onto your saucepan (this not only frees up your hands but also keeps the end of the thermometer from sitting on the bottom of the pot and giving a false reading). Personally, I use a temperature gun, as it can very quickly grab the temperature at different spots around the pot. You want to check the temperature at different spots and average the reading to be the most accurate.

Kitchen torch

For pie making, this is a tool that really only has one use, but it is really fun to watch the perfect meringue peaks turn a golden brown as the flame kisses them, and you feel pretty badass using it! You can pick up one of these little culinary torches relatively inexpensively, and who knows? You may then be inclined to make crème brûlée as well.

Pastry brush

A pastry brush is used to apply the wash to the top of a double-crust pie and around the edges to help seal the pie shut. For the most coverage, I find that a traditional bristle (rather than silicone) pastry brush works best. A brand-new brush might shed a few bristles, so keep an eye out during the first couple of uses, but once broken in, they are great. They do require some TLC for the cleanup: hand wash the brush very thoroughly (I recommend hand washing only, as the heat from the dishwasher can dissolve the glue and ruin the brush) to remove all the egg, and dry the brush well to keep the metal band from rusting.

Pie crimper

I love this tool. I find it useful for multiple applications in pie making. It might not always be the easiest tool to track down, but some specialty cookware shops carry them. The pie crimper is a little wheel that can cut the pastry to create a pretty little wavy line. We use it most often in our bakery to help seal handpies shut. The one I like best is a single wheel that has a blunt wavy edge. Other pie crimpers can have two wheels with different edges for different cuts. The blade on the latter is a little sharper and I find it great to cut the pastry, but a blunt edge works best for sealing.

Knives & peelers

Making pies can involve prepping both fruit and vegetables. Having good-quality sharp knives and peelers is important, and will make the job safer and easier. You need a good chef's knife to dice veggies for the savory pies and a paring knife for cleaning up the fruits or peeling apples if you do not have a peeler.

Scissors

Scissors might not be a common tool for most people when making pies, but we use them in our bakery all the time to trim the excess dough from around the pie before fluting the edge. I thank my mom for this, as in her kitchen she used scissors for just about everything. You don't need to get any special kind of scissors, just a basic pair will do, but have them dedicated to the kitchen only to keep them sanitary.

Ingredients

Butter

It is my opinion that butter is the single most important ingredient when it comes to making pie. The basis of the pie is the crust—this is what separates a great pie from a mediocre pie—and in my humble opinion, butter makes the tastiest, flakiest, to-die-for crust. When selecting butter, make sure to pick unsalted. This way you control the amount of salt that goes into your recipe.

There are so many different brands of butter on the market to choose from. Different brands have different fat content, so check the package to make sure it has a high fat content. I encourage you to buy a few different brands and spend a day testing them out in your pastry to get to know your favorite. This will take some time, but once you know, you know! Over the years I have tried a lot of different butters to find the very best for crust. Even after all these years, I feel obligated when a sales rep comes into the bakery with butter, to give it a shot. I take their butter, our butter, and a few other brands I pick to act as controls in my pie crust experiments. Once I have them all baked, we gather all the staff to try them in a blind taste test. My bakers are always able to tell which one uses our butter.

Flour

The flour we use in our bakery is always unbleached all-purpose flour, as this means less processing and therefore fewer additives. Over the years, I have experimented with different types of flour. I love the idea of locally milled heirloom grains, but while I find they make amazing cookies and cakes, it just hasn't worked for our pie crust.

Sugar & salt

Our signature Double Butter Crust is used for 90 percent of our pies, whether sweet or savory. So you might be surprised to find sugar in the crust of a chicken pot pie, but I find that pie dough needs a slight touch of sweetness and saltiness so it doesn't come across as dull. We use a basic white granulated sugar and a fine sea salt.

Water

Tap water is fine for this. The key is to keep the water cold. The addition of an ice cube or two, especially on a hot summer day, is definitely a good idea. Before we start making our pastry, we always measure the water and vinegar first, and set them in the bakery fridge, which we keep colder than average.

Vinegar

Vinegar is an important part of making our Double Butter Crust. The addition of acid helps to prevent gluten formation and dough oxidation. We chose white table vinegar because it is easily accessible, is inexpensive, bakes with no flavor, doesn't change the color, and gets the job done. Other acids can be used, like orange juice or lemon juice, but both impart flavor, so we like the versatility of vinegar best. Other recipes suggest using vodka, but in my experience this can make your dough a little harder to work with, and no one wants to be frustrated making pie. I recommend using that vodka to mix yourself a Cosmo and have a little fun while baking.

About the Recipes

In the list of recipes at the start of each chapter, you'll see letters attached to some of the recipes. Here's the cheat sheet of what they mean:

V = VEGAN (or easily adapted to vegan if you substitute the vegan pie crust recipe on page 25 and organic cane sugar for regular sugar).

GF = GLUTEN-FREE.

AW = AWARD-WINNING! These are our pies for the record books.

And for ingredients, please note that unless it says otherwise:

BUTTER = UNSALTED
FLOUR = ALL-PURPOSE
SALT = KOSHER
MILK = WHOLE
PEPPER = FRESHLY CRACKED BLACK
SUGAR = WHITE GRANULATED

Types of Pies

When it comes to making pies, there are infinite fillings and toppings to try, but there are really only two basic kinds of pie.

Single-crust pies

These have a bottom crust only. This might be made of a traditional pastry, like our Double Butter Crust (page 20), or have a pressed crust (pages 36 to 42) using graham crumbs, cookies, nuts, etc. (Really, if you can crush it and add butter to it, you can press it!) Single-crust pies are typically cream pies, curd pies, and crumbles. Some single-crust pies have to be partially or fully prebaked before the filling is added (read more about this on page 29).

Double-crust pies

These have two crusts, a bottom and a top. The bottom crust is treated the same way as in a single-crust pie; the top crust helps protect the filling from burning in the oven (and also tastes great!). Double-crust pies are most common with fruit pies and savory pies. Not all double-crust pies have a full top— you can make a beautiful lattice or herringbone instead or almost any other decorative design. See pages 30 to 35 for ideas on making a jaw-dropping-gorgeous pie.

Rolling in the Dough

It always surprises me when people tell me that they think making pie is hard, and I have to remind myself that when I started I had that same fear. I'd always loved baking but shied away from pie because of the reputation the crust had for being difficult to make. Then I thought, how hard can it really be? There are only a few ingredients involved after all; it's really just cutting fat into flour. I started out by using the crust recipe on the back of a package of lard—no shame in that; we all have to start somewhere!—but then my sister encouraged me to develop my own recipe. If the fillings of my pies were all my own recipes, why should the crust be any different? That's when I left the lard behind to go with all butter. I started with some butter, then more butter, and then more butter and more (double the amount in most recipes!) until I found pie crust perfection. Hence the name Double Butter Crust (see the recipe on page 20).

By hand (page 20)

My first choice is to make pie dough by hand. When I first started The Pie Hole I had this stubborn belief that each batch had to be made by my own hands. I just love the feeling of the dough in my fingers, and the control that comes from that. My heart tells me you get a better result (even if blind taste tests in our bakery have told me otherwise!). I know the love that goes into the dough while I gently roll the butter in through my fingertips.

Stand mixer (page 22)

The third option is using a stand mixer fitted with the paddle attachment. This is how we make our batches of dough at the bakery now, as we use 20 pounds of butter in each batch and a large 60-quart mixer! You can easily make dough with your stand mixer at home. On low speed, the paddle pushes the butter around slowly, breaking it down into small pieces and coating it with the dry ingredients with each turn of the mixer.

Food processor (page 22)

As The Pie Hole grew, I had little choice but to move away from individual handmade batches of dough and start using a food processor to make larger batches to keep up with the demand. When using a food processor you have to be careful, as the risk of overmixing the dough is high. Use very short pulses and wait for the mixture to have that crumbly look and loosely come together.

note You can make your dough up to three days ahead and keep it tightly wrapped in the fridge. Any longer than that and you'll want to freeze the dough; it lasts for up to 3 months in the freezer.

FEELING CRUSTY?

To have a great pie, you need to start from the bottom up. Whether it is rolled or pressed, the crust is the foundation that holds all the goodness that comes on top. All amazing things start with a solid foundation, which is why we are starting the recipes in this book with the crusts!

In this chapter are nine different pie crust recipes for you to give a whirl. In each of the individual pie recipes later in the book, I specify whether you need a single or double crust for the pie, and which particular crust I recommend. Don't feel that you need to be beholden to my recommendations though—you can always mix it up and try a different filling with a different crust. And there's also no shame in buying premade pastry or pie crust and loading it up with the good stuff! Although, truth be told, once you taste my Double Butter Crust (page 20), there's really no going back.

The crust of a pie should never take the back seat and simply be the vessel—a vessel that far too often gets left on the plate while the "good stuff" gets eaten. So I made it my mission to develop the most delicious, buttery, flaky crust possible. We use so much butter in fact that we call our pastry Double Butter Crust. And let me tell you, we have all the flavor and all the flakes!

DOUBLE BUTTER CRUST

MAKES ONE 9-INCH DOUBLE CRUST (OR TWO 9-INCH SINGLE CRUSTS)

1 cup (250 mL) water, ice cold

1 Tbsp vinegar, cold

2 cups (454 g) butter, cold

4 cups (600 g) flour

2 Tbsp sugar

1 tsp salt

Egg wash (page 43)

> **note** The amount of water mixture you need will vary each time you make the dough. A number of variables contribute to this, including the moisture content in the flour (influenced by how the flour is stored), the warmth of your hands, the time of year, and how hot or cold your kitchen is. You will most likely not use all of the water mixture, but it's better to have a little too much than not enough. And don't fret if there is a little extra flour in the bottom of the bowl.

1. Start by mixing the water and vinegar together in a bowl or jug and putting it into the freezer so it's icy cold when you need it. Cut the butter into 1-inch cubes and put them in the freezer too to keep as cold as possible while you measure the other ingredients.

Prepare the dough by hand

1. Measure the flour, sugar, and salt into a large mixing bowl and mix to fully incorporate.

2. Add the cold butter to the flour mixture, and use your fingers to massage the butter into the flour, breaking it apart and coating it in flour. Continue massaging and rolling the butter between your fingers until you have a coarse mixture with pea- to almond-sized pieces of butter throughout.

3. Add 3 Tbsp of the cold vinegar-water mixture. Slowly mix in the water with your hands, gently squeezing the butter and flour to help it come together.

4. Continue adding the vinegar-water mixture just 1 Tbsp at a time, mixing it in gently with your hands. The goal is to add just enough water to get the dough to come together into a shaggy mixture —and once it gets to that point, hands off (see Note on page 22)!

5. Turn to chill the dough on page 22 for directions on how to chill and roll your dough.

Or prepare the dough by food processor

1. In a food processor, pulse the flour, sugar, and salt until mixed. A few quick pulses should do it. Add the cold butter, a few pieces at a time, pulsing until you have a coarse mixture with pea- to almond-sized pieces of butter throughout. Do not overmix! It's very easy to overmix, so be careful.

2. Add 3 Tbsp of the cold vinegar-water mixture. Pulse a few times. Continue to add vinegar and water, 1 Tbsp at a time, pulsing a few times between each addition. The goal is to add just enough water to get the dough to come together into a shaggy mixture—and once it gets to that point, no more pulsing (see Note)!

3. Transfer to a floured work surface, and carefully fold any loose bits of flour and butter into the ball of dough. Folding it a few times will create layers. Next, read below for how to chill the dough.

Or prepare the dough by stand mixer

1. Using a stand mixer fitted with the paddle attachment, combine the flour, sugar, and salt on low speed.

2. With the mixer running on low speed, add the cold butter, a few pieces at a time, mixing until you have a coarse mixture with pea- to almond-sized pieces of butter throughout. Do not overmix.

3. With the mixer still running on low speed, add 3 Tbsp of the cold vinegar-water mixture. Continue to add vinegar and water, 1 Tbsp at a time, mixing for 30 seconds between each addition. The goal is to add just enough water to get the dough to come together into a shaggy mixture—and once it gets to that point, stop mixing (see Note)! I find that using a stand mixer takes the most practice and that it is easy to add too much water if you are not patient.

4. Once the dough just comes together, remove it from the mixing bowl, cleaning off the paddle so as not to miss out on any of the delicious buttery dough. Next, read below for how to chill the dough.

Then, chill the dough

1. Bring your dough together to form a ball, divide it in half, and wrap each piece snugly with plastic wrap. At this point the dough is quite pliable, so press it down until it forms disks about 1 inch thick. This will save both time and effort when you start rolling the dough, as it's more difficult to roll once chilled. Place the disks in the fridge for a minimum of 30 minutes to relax the gluten in the dough, which gives you a much more tender pastry. At this point you can also freeze the dough.

Rolling the dough

1. When you are ready to start rolling, remove the dough from the fridge and unwrap it (you need 1 disk for a single-crust pie and 2 disks for a double-crust pie). If the dough is frozen, fully thaw it first (by moving it to the fridge overnight, or sitting it out on the counter for a couple of hours).

2. Sprinkle your work surface and dough with flour , and use a rolling pin to start rolling out 1 of the disks. Rotate the dough 90 degrees after every few passes to work toward creating a circular shape. If the circumference of the disk is not getting larger as you roll, there's a good chance the dough is stuck to the surface below. Carefully lift the dough and add more flour to the surface. I also often flour the top of the dough and flip it over, then continue to roll. Keep rolling out the dough until it is about ⅛ inch thick.

3. Next, take your pie plate and turn it upside down in the center of the rolled dough. Use the plate as a template to cut the dough to size. Depending on the depth of the pie plate, cut out a circle of dough 1½ to 2 inches larger than the rim of the pie plate (the deeper the pie plate, the larger the circle will need to be). It is best to go larger, as you can always trim; you never want to have to stretch the dough to make it fit, as it shrinks back as it bakes.

4. Remove the pie plate and sprinkle a little flour over the surface of the dough. Then gently lift and transfer the dough to the pie plate with the floured side facing down. This, along with all the butter in the dough, will help keep the pie from sticking to the pie plate, so no need to worry about greasing or flouring your pie plate. Gently press the dough into the plate.

5. Dock the bottom of the dough with a fork to allow steam to escape when baking.

Next, for a single-crust pie

1. If you have more than ¼-inch overhang of dough, trim the excess with scissors, and finish the pie with a fluted edge. *Tip: Create a fluted edge by pushing a little of the dough out with your thumb at the same time as pulling back the dough beside it with your index finger, squeezing and bending the dough between your fingertips to create an exaggerated fluted edge. Use the index finger on your opposite hand as a spacer between each flute for consistency.*

2. Use a pastry brush to brush the edges of the pie with egg wash (see page 43). Make sure to get it into all the nooks and crannies to achieve a consistent perfect golden color all over. If the crust requires blind baking, do that now (see page 24).

3. Keep chilled until you are ready to assemble the pie. Follow the individual pie recipe for next steps on filling, baking, and serving the pie. Yum!

Or, for a double-crust pie

1. Repeat steps 1 and 2 of Rolling the Dough with your second disk of dough. If you are creating a full lid for your top pie crust, try to roll the dough into an even circular shape. If you are preparing the dough for a lattice design (see page 30) try to roll it into more of a rectangular shape to help you cut nice even strips that will fit across the pie without stretching. Keep chilled until you are ready to assemble the pie.

2. Once you have added the pie filling to the bottom crust, use a pastry brush to brush the edges of the crust with egg wash. Make sure to get it into all the nooks and crannies as this helps the top pie crust to adhere to it.

3. Top with the top pie crust and secure the edges by pinching the bottom and top crusts together. Trim off any excess dough and flute the edges (see Tip in single-crust pie method on page 23). Brush the whole surface with egg wash. Follow the individual pie recipe for baking and serving the pie. Double crust, double yum!

For blind baking

1. Preheat the oven to 350°F.

2. Line the inside of the prepared pie crust with parchment paper to protect the dough. *Tip: Large coffee filters can also be used here instead.* Add pie weights (see page 8) to keep the pastry in place, and so the heat of the oven doesn't just melt the pastry into a buttery puddle in the bottom of the pie plate.

3. Bake in the oven for 20 to 25 minutes. Remove from the oven, but keep the oven on. Remove the weights and parchment paper and brush the base of the pie crust with egg wash.

4. For a fully blind-baked pie, return to the oven for 8 to 10 minutes; for a partially blind-baked pie, return to the oven for 3 to 5 minutes. This cooks the additional egg wash and creates a barrier between the filling and the crust to keep the crust from becoming soggy.

t has always been important to create a recipe that I am truly proud of. When people ask if we do a gluten-free pie, I have to tell them we don't. And it is not for lack of trying. I have never been able to crack the code of really good gluten-free pastry. A vegan pastry on the other hand? No problem! So many pie crusts are actually already vegan as many vegetable shortenings are vegan. Many of our fillings are easily converted to vegan just by using the right sugar and this crust recipe. We are delighted to be able to offer plant-based options in our shops.

VEGAN PIE CRUST

MAKES ONE 9-INCH DOUBLE CRUST (OR TWO 9-INCH SINGLE CRUSTS)

1 cup (250 mL) water, ice cold

2 Tbsp vinegar

1⅓ cup (295 g) vegan butter, cold

¾ cup (130 g) vegan shortening, cold

5 cups (750 g) flour

2 Tbsp organic cane sugar

1 tsp salt

1. Mix the water and vinegar together in a bowl or jug and put it into the freezer so it's icy cold when you need it.

2. Cut the vegan butter into 1-inch cubes, and chill in the freezer. As the vegan shortening is too soft to cut, use a tablespoon to scoop pieces about 1 inch across. Place in the freezer too to keep as cold as possible.

3. Measure the flour, sugar, and salt into a large mixing bowl and mix to fully incorporate.

4. Add the cold vegan butter and vegan shortening to the flour mixture, and gently use your fingers to massage them into the flour, breaking the pieces apart and coating them in flour. Continue massaging and rolling the butter between your fingers until you have a coarse mixture with pea- to almond-sized pieces of butter and shortening throughout. Do not overmix.

5. Turn to chill the dough on page 22, and then follow the remaining steps on pages 23 and 24 to roll the dough and finish the crust.

hile there is some science behind why my dough works so well, I was never great at science growing up, so let me just give you a quick rundown of my best tips and tricks for achieving a killer crust.

Tips & Tricks for the Perfect Crust

COLD, COLD, COLD! The first thing is, and I simply cannot stress this enough, keeping the butter you use as cold as possible. How to do this? Stay hands off! The more you handle your dough, the more the butter warms up, so when you reach that perfect crumbly texture—hands off! Your pie crust will work much better if you keep things as cold as possible. Keep your water and vinegar cold too. We keep ours in the fridge until it is time to add to the mixture. On really hot summer days, you can also add an ice cube to the water.

ADD ACID Speaking of vinegar, there are a lot of different reasons why, but adding acid (for us this is always vinegar) to the ice water for your dough will help give you an amazing pastry. Some say it helps prevent gluten formation, making the dough more tender and flaky; others say it helps prevent oxidation to keep the color from becoming dull and grayish. Whatever the reason, we use it—every batch of dough has some vinegar in it and it works very well for us.

HANDS OFF! I see this in every class I teach: you get your dough mixed to that perfect shaggy state where it is just coming together, but something keeps drawing you back to the bowl to keep working the dough! Please try as hard as you can to resist, as this will lengthen the gluten strands in the pastry and result in a tough dough. If you have extra flour left over, that's totally fine—the consistency is the most important thing. Also, you never want to knead your dough; pie is not bread. Instead, work fast and bring the dough together by folding the dough onto itself helps create the beautiful buttery layers.

CHILL YOUR DOUGH Once you have finished making your dough, it is important to let it rest in the fridge for at least 30 minutes. This gives the flour time to properly absorb all the water and gives the gluten time to relax. This will give you pie dough that is easy to roll out.

Before chilling, wrap the dough in plastic wrap. It will still be pliable at this time, so press it into a disk shape with the palms of your hands. This will make your life so much easier when the time comes to roll the dough out. Flatten the disk to about an inch thick and chill in the fridge for an absolute minimum of 30 minutes (longer if you planned ahead and have the time). If your pie crust shrinks during baking, there is a strong chance you didn't rest and chill the dough long enough.

ROLLING, ROLLING, ROLLING Sprinkle your work surface with a little flour first. In the warmer months, to help keep the dough from sticking to the table or the rolling pin you can add a little extra. If you notice that your dough is not getting thin enough and the diameter is not increasing, it is probably stuck to the table. So add a little more flour (but not too much as this can change the fat to flour ratio and make your dough tough).

When you are rolling, lifting and moving the dough around is good. If you are forcing the shape by stretching and pulling the dough rather than rolling, you will notice the difference when you bake your pie, when it shrinks back and leaves you with an uneven shape.

The same applies to placing the dough in the pie plate. Make sure you have more than enough hanging over the edges. You can always trim away the excess—stretching it might seem like a good idea and it might look good as it goes into the oven, but it will shrink as it bakes and you will have a pie with shrunken sides. Always be gentle with your dough; it appreciates a soft touch.

DOCKING You always need to dock the bottom pie crust with a fork. Docking is the term used to describe perforating the pie dough with the tines of a fork. This allows the steam to escape and prevents the crust from forming air pockets (which mean less filling and sad customers). Err on the side of too much docking as this will cause no harm.

FINISHING YOUR PIE Finish your pie (and I don't mean eating it, that's easy!) with a decorative edge. My favorite, and what 90 percent of the pies at the shop have, is a fluted edge. Some bakers take the bottom and the top crust and roll them over to work with a smooth rolled edge, but my Double Butter Crust builds layers into the pastry with all the butter, and I think it is a shame to hide those layers. There are a number of different ways to flute (the Tip on page 23 explains how I do it), each as personal as your signature. When I look at the pies in the shop, some of the fluted edges are so distinctive that I know exactly who made them. You can also finish your pie in classic Grandma style (doing it Grandma style is sealing the pie with the tines of a fork) or use cookie cutters to cut out any shapes you like, like leaves, or half circles, or a ring of hearts to line around the edge of the pie (see page 34). Or turn to page 32 for how to beautifully braid dough to wrap around the circumference of the pie.

SCRUB-A-DUB-DUB: TIME FOR A WASH
"Washing" the top of a pie adds to the visual aesthetic of the pie by browning the crust and creating a shine. The wash can also help seal the edges of double-crust pies, handpies, pop tarts, pie pops, and so on. At The Pie Hole we prefer a straight-up egg wash (see page 43) because of its neutral flavor and the way it

notes These may seem obvious, but I once had a roommate who didn't remove the plastic shrink-wrap from a frozen pizza before putting it in the oven, so I don't assume anything is obvious anymore:

• Always preheat your oven before baking pie.

• Use oven mitts to remove the pie from the oven.

• Cool the pie to the recipe's specifications before you eat it or decorate it.

browns a pie to perfection. You can also switch it up and use milk, olive oil, or plant-based milks (page 43). Each gives a slightly different appearance due to the protein level of the wash, and imparts a different flavor, which might be exactly what you are looking for.

CHILL IT AGAIN! Before your pie goes in the oven, it is a very good idea to chill the assembled pie for 30 minutes in the fridge or 15 minutes in the freezer. This way the butter in the pastry is super cold when it goes into the oven. As the butter melts, the water in the butter evaporates, turning to steam, which helps to separate the layers in the dough, giving the flakiness that has become synonymous with the perfect pie crust.

BAKE IT BLIND! Blind baking is when you prebake (either partially or fully) the pie crust before you add the pie filling. Whether blind baking is necessary or not depends on the filling. Some fillings (like Key Lime Pie, page 219, or To Die for Banana Cream Pie, page 171) need only a short baking time just to set the filling and no more—so a partial blind bake first ensures that the crust will be cooked to perfection at the same time that the filling is ready. Other pie fillings require no baking time at all (like Lemon Meringue Pie, page 217, and Coconut Cream Pie, page 181)—for those you want a complete blind bake before filling.

Pie Problems Solved

What if your pie comes out of the oven with a soggy bottom? No one likes a soggy bottom! There are a few reasons why this can happen:

1. The crust is rolled too thick, and it doesn't bake fully. SOLUTION: Make sure you keep it at only ⅛ inch thick.

2. The pie plate has too thick a bottom and the heat cannot get through to fully cook the crust. SOLUTION: Slide a pizza stone under the pie plate while it is baking.

3. The filling is super juicy (most common with berry pies).SOLUTION: Use our "B"airy Dust on page 255.

4. The pie is too high in the oven and bakes too quickly. SOLUTION: Always position your pie on the middle rack.

5. The oven temperature is too low. SOLUTION: Follow the recipe and make sure the oven is fully preheated first.

wanted to dedicate a section of this book to pie art and encourage you to try to make a pie that you will be so proud of. You can spend as much or as little time as you have.

Vincent Van Dough: Pie Art

LATTICE GET FANCY

Making a woven lattice top may seem like a difficult task, but trust me it is not that hard, and the end result is so worth the extra 5 or 10 minutes. You can vary the size of the lattice strips from super thin to very thick, keep them all uniform in size, or use a combination of sizes on a single pie. The spacing can be very tight or you can spread the lattice out to give a peek-a-boo of the filling inside. Of course the purpose of the lattice, or any pie top, is to first and foremost protect the filling; but if it happens to look amazing in the meantime, even better!

MAKES A LATTICE CRUST FOR ONE 9-INCH PIE

½ recipe Double Butter Crust dough (page 20)

note Always take pictures of your beautiful pie before it goes in the oven. You never know what will happen with a super-flaky pastry and fresh fruit!.

1. Start with chilled pie dough and roll to approximately ⅛ inch thick. Using a pastry roller, a paring knife, or even a pizza cutter, cut the strips for the lattice. The size is completely up to you; just remember that the thinner the strips are, the more you need and the more difficult it becomes to lay them. I like my strips to be about 1 inch thick and use 10 strips to cover a 9-inch pie.

2. Use a pastry brush to brush around the edge of the bottom crust as this will be the glue that holds the lattice strips in place once they are all laid. As you lay the strips, do not push them into this edge until they are all in place as they will stick and make the process much harder.

3. Start by making a cross across the top of the pie. Then lay 2 strips over the strip that is on top and perpendicular.

4. Carefully fold back the strip that is between the 2 you just laid and place another strip parallel to the perpendicular strip. Fold the first strip back overtop. Do this on both sides.

5. Continue to fold back the strips that are under the top laid strip and adding more strips until the pie is completely covered.

6. Pinch the strips down to connect them to the bottom crust edge. Trim the excess ends off and flute the pie.

BRAIDED CRUST

Braids can look so pretty on pies, whether it is a fully braided lattice top, a single or double braid slipped in amid the regular lattice top, or a braided ring around the circumference of the pie. Take a look at the photos on page iv and 35 for inspiration! A key point to note when braiding: you need your strips to be much longer than the intended size of the final braid. It can be discouraging when you put the work in and end up with a super-short braid that doesn't fit on your pie. It is better to err on the safe side and make a braid that is too long and can be trimmed. The amount of dough you need depends on the size and number of braids.

1. Start with chilled pie dough and roll it into a long, thin rectangle, about 16 inches wide and approximately ⅛ inch thick. Using a pastry roller, a paring knife, or even a pizza cutter, cut the dough into 3 long thin strips, each ¼ inch thick. Make sure the strips are the same width and length.
2. Start by pinching the 3 strips together at the top and laying them flat on your work surface.
3. Take the strip on the far right and gently pull and lay it across the middle strip. Then take the strip from the far left and bring it across the middle strip.
4. Continue this process until you reach the bottom of the strips. You can pull these as tight as you would like or leave them loose. This comes down to personal preference.

PIE ROSES

Little pastry roses might be one of the easiest things to make and the most effective for embellishing a pie top. You can vary the size of the roses by picking different diameter circle cutters. I find that 1-inch circles are the perfect size. The amount of dough you need depends on the number of roses you plan to make; usually I just re-roll whatever scraps I have on hand. Take a look at the photo on page iv.

1. Start with chilled pie dough and roll it out to approximately ⅛ inch thick. Using a 1-inch circle cookie cutter, cut out 5 circles of dough per rose.
2. Start by laying the circles on your work surface. Use a pastry brush to brush 1 side with egg wash. Place the second circle just overlapping on top of the first and press down gently in place. Repeat with the 3 other circles of dough. You do not want to have too many layers or the rose will be too thick and the middle will not bake properly. I like to use 5 thinly rolled pastry circles to make my roses.
3. Very carefully start at the end of the circle that is underneath and roll toward the other end. Once rolled, pinch in the middle and give a little squeeze to encourage the rose shape. Cut in half, creating 2 roses. Use your thumbs to gently peel the petals back to give the rose its full appearance.
4. Repeat for the number of roses you desire.

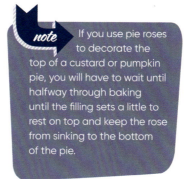

note If you use pie roses to decorate the top of a custard or pumpkin pie, you will have to wait until halfway through baking until the filling sets a little to rest on top and keep the rose from sinking to the bottom of the pie.

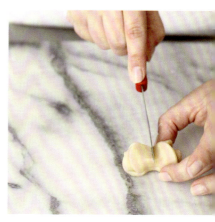

Cheeky Sayings

You can't really call your company The Pie Hole without having a cheeky side. Over the years we have put some pretty fun sayings on our pies, especially messages for Valentine's Day, like "I Only Have Pies For You." Recently, we opened it up to our customers to pick their own sayings. Some cute, some sassy, and some wildly inappropriate came to us—and, yes, we even had a marriage proposal!

Keep it cold

When working on fine details with pastry the key is keeping it as cold as possible. It is easier to cut out small details when the dough is very cold. I always put a nicely rolled sheet of pie dough on a baking sheet and into the freezer for 15 minutes before cutting details and stamping out shapes with cookie cutters. If the dough starts to get too warm you can always throw it back in again to chill.

Try not to move decorative/cutout pieces very much. The more you handle them, the more they will deform while baking. Use a tool like a bench scraper to transfer your designs to the pie.

Cut-out letters

Pick up a set of small alphabet cutters that work well for pie pastry. I find to achieve the most legible message, you should stick cut-out letters to the top crust, using the egg wash as glue. You can also cut out the letters directly from the top crust, but as you flute the pie, and as it bakes, the letters tend to get distorted.

One other thing to be mindful of, especially if you are using our Double Butter Crust, is that the first time you roll the dough it is very flaky and puffs up. For detailed letters and shapes, I recommend that you use the scrap dough that has been worked a little more and won't puff up as much.

Steady hand

In addition to lettering, there are so many other ways to decorate a pie. Most decorating I do by hand and I love to take advantage of every seasonal opportunity! It takes patience to do things free hand, but the payoff is worth it. As always, start with very cold dough. Use a very sharp paring knife or a penknife to cut your desired shapes. Avoid dragging the knife through the dough as this can pull and distort the design. If you are planning very tiny details, hold the blade perpendicular to the dough and quickly poke it into the dough like a sewing machine needle. This will create you tight perforations so you can easily separate out the pieces. Use egg wash as a glue to attach the desired shapes to each other and to the pie to get your final design. Freeze the pie for a minimum of 30 minutes *before* baking, to give the dough the best chance of holding its shape. And *always* take a picture of your masterpiece before baking; baked pie can be a beautiful, unpredictable mess at times.

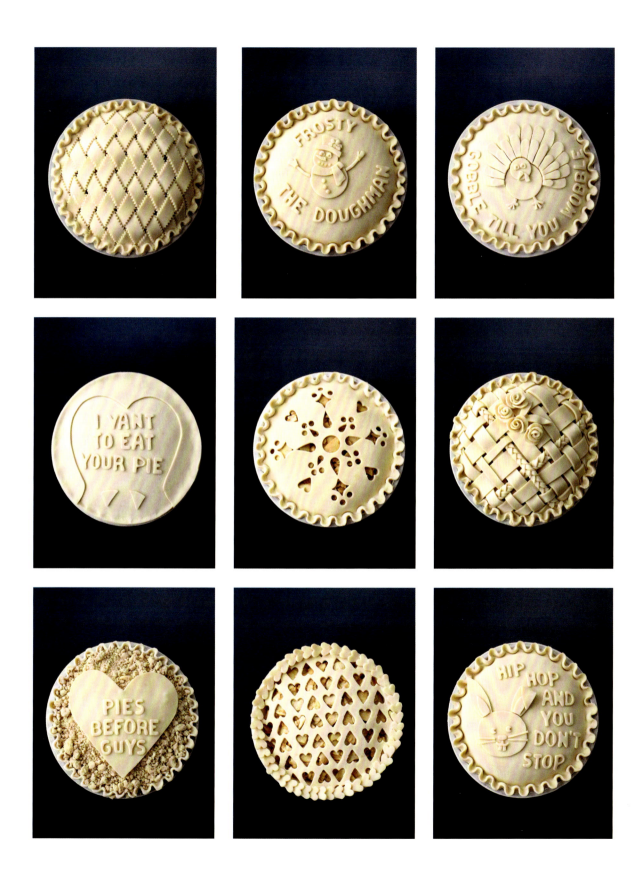

As a kid, my favorite part of store-bought cream pies was the graham crust. I often just dug through the creamy filling to find that golden graham crust at the bottom of the pie. .

Pressed Crusts

note All pressed pie crusts can be stored in the fridge for up to 3 days or the freezer for up to 3 months.

GRAHAM CRACKER CRUST

Graham crust is a must for Key Lime Pie (page 219), and when the mood strikes, you can use it for To Die for Banana Cream Pie (page 171).

MAKES ONE 9-INCH PIE SHELL

½ cup (114 g) butter

2¾ cups (360 g) honey graham crumbs

3 Tbsp sugar

Pinch salt

1. Preheat the oven to 350°F.

2. Melt the butter in a small saucepan or a microwave-safe dish.

3. Measure the honey graham crumbs, sugar, and salt into a large mixing bowl and mix to fully incorporate. Add the melted butter and use a spatula to thoroughly mix until the mixture has the consistency of wet sand and holds together when squeezed.

4. Transfer the crumbs to a 9-inch pie plate. Using your hands or the bottom of a flat measuring cup or glass, push down the crumbs to neatly and evenly line the bottom and sides of the pie plate.

5. Bake for 7 minutes if you need the crust partially prebaked and 15 minutes if you need it fully blind baked. Allow the pie shell to cool completely before filling it.

PEANUT GRAHAM CRACKER CRUST

This creates the perfect base for the Peanut Butter Cup Pie (page 163) and even a nice change-up for our ever-so-popular Fat Elvis Pie (page 160).

As above plus:

⅓ cup (45 g) chopped peanuts (unsalted or dry roasted)

1. Before you melt the butter, pulse the peanuts in a food processor until you have a fine crumb mixture. Be careful not to pulse too much or you will end up with peanut butter.

2. Add the finely ground peanuts when you add the honey graham crumbs, reducing the measure of honey graham crumbs slightly to 2¼ cups (290 g).

GLUTEN-FREE GRAHAM CRUMB CRUST

While we don't do a gluten-free traditional pie dough at The Pie Hole, we do make our own gluten-free graham crackers to create this crust. You can pair this crust with quite a few of our pie fillings that are already gluten-free, like Key Lime Pie (page 219), Coconut Cream Pie (page 181), and the ooey gooey S'More Pie (page 207).

MAKES TWO 9-INCH PIE SHELLS

Gluten-Free Graham Crackers

1½ cups (240 g) gluten-free flour (I use Bob's Red Mill)

½ cup (75 g) almond meal

½ cup (100 g) golden sugar

¼ cup (40 g) xanthan gum

2 tsp baking powder

1 tsp cinnamon

½ tsp salt

7 Tbsp (100 g) butter, cold

3 Tbsp water

2 Tbsp honey

1 tsp vanilla

Crust

3 Tbsp butter

2 Tbsp sugar

For the gluten-free graham crackers

1. Add the flour, almond meal, golden sugar, xanthan gum, baking powder, cinnamon, and salt into a large mixing bowl and mix to fully incorporate. Add the butter and use your fingers to massage the butter into the flour, breaking it apart and coating it in flour. Continue massaging and rolling the butter between your fingers until you have a texture like coarse sand.

2. Make a small well in the center of the dry ingredients and add the water, honey, and vanilla to the center. Using a spatula, mix the wet ingredients, then pull the dry ingredients into the wet and continue to mix until the dough comes together.

3. Bring your dough together to form a disk and wrap it snugly with plastic wrap. At this point the dough is quite pliable, so I like to take the dough and press it down until it forms a disk about 1 inch thick. This will save both time and effort when you start rolling the dough, as it's more difficult to roll once chilled. Place the disk in the fridge for 30 minutes.

4. Preheat the oven to 350°F. Line a baking sheet with parchment paper.

5. Sprinkle your work surface with gluten-free flour, and use a rolling pin to start rolling out the dough into a large rectangle. Continue rolling out the dough until it is ¼ inch thick. Transfer to the prepared baking sheet. Using a fork, dock the rolled dough to help keep it flat while baking. Bake for 25 to 30 minutes, until golden brown. Remove from the oven and allow to cool.

6. Once cool, chop one-third of the sheet into cracker-sized pieces. These can be stored in an airtight container for up to 1 week. Chop up the remaining two-thirds and transfer to a large resealable plastic bag. Use a rolling pin to crush them. Transfer to a large mixing bowl. You can also pulse in a food processor to turn to a crumb.

For the crust

1. Melt the butter in a small saucepan or a microwave-safe dish. Add the melted butter and the sugar to the cracker crumbs and mix well to combine.

2. Transfer the crumbly mixture to a 9-inch pie plate. Using your hands or the bottom of a flat measuring cup or drinking cup, push down the crumbs to neatly and evenly line the bottom of the pie plate.

3. Bake for 7 minutes if you need the crust partially prebaked and 15 minutes if you need it fully prebaked. Allow the pie shell to cool completely before filling it.

VEGAN COCONUT WALNUT CRUST

This is our only raw vegan crust, and it is so good! It happens to also be very easy to make. Just throw a handful of good, whole ingredients into the food processor and voilà, you have the makings for our Vegan Avocado Key Lime Pie (page 220).

MAKES ONE 9-INCH PIE SHELL

1⅔ cups (150 g) unsweetened shredded coconut

1½ cups (180 g) whole walnuts

1½ cups (300 g) pitted dates

1 tsp lime zest

Pinch sea salt

note Press the mixture into an 8-by-8-inch cake pan to make a base for delicious bars.

1. In a food processor, pulse the shredded coconut and walnuts until the mixture has a coarse, crumbly consistency. Add the dates, lime zest, and salt and pulse until the mixture has an even crumbly consistency and is thoroughly combined.

2. Transfer the mixture to a 9-inch pie plate. Using your hands or the bottom of a flat measuring cup or glass, push down the crumbs to neatly and evenly line the bottom and sides of the pie plate.

3. As this is a raw pie crust, you are done! Keep it in the fridge while you make the filling.

VEGAN HAZELNUT CRUMB CRUST

This pressed crust is so addictive I always roll the extra into little truffle-like balls for snacks. Take a look at the ingredients; this crust is actually pretty healthy and definitely delicious! We only use this crust for one pie in our shops, the Vegan Chocolate Hazelnut Pie (page 167), but you could easily get creative and come up with some other delicious fillings (think banana!).

MAKES ONE 9-INCH PIE SHELL

1 cup (110 g) rolled oats

1½ cups (220 g) whole skinned hazelnuts

1½ cups (115 g) unsweetened shredded coconut

¼ cup (30 g) cocoa powder

¼ tsp salt

3 Tbsp coconut oil, melted

⅓ cup (80 mL) maple syrup

1. Preheat the oven to 350°F.

2. In a food processor, blend the oats until they are a coarse powder. Add the hazelnuts and blend until you have a fine, crumbly texture. Add the shredded coconut, cocoa powder, and salt. Pulse to mix thoroughly while keeping the crumb-like consistency.

3. Add the melted coconut oil and maple syrup and pulse until these ingredients are incorporated and the mixture has a consistency like wet sand and holds together when squeezed.

4. Transfer the wet, crumbly mixture to a 9-inch pie plate. Using damp hands or the bottom of a flat measuring cup or glass, push down the crumbs to neatly and evenly line the bottom and sides of the pie plate. Dock the bottom of the crust by using a fork to prick the crust to the bottom of the plate.

5. Bake for 10 to 12 minutes, until the crust is no longer shiny. If the base of the crust has puffed up during baking, carefully push it back down (caution: it will be hot!). Let the crust cool completely before filling.

Candy Bar Crust

Dark Chocolate Crumb Crust

Graham Cracker Crust

> **note** That's the way the cookie crumbles! Use a food processor to grind your graham crackers, cookies, nuts etc. as fine as possible. The finer the grind, the tighter the crust and the better it will hold.

Gluten-free Graham Cracker Crust

Peanut Graham Cracker Crust

Nanaimo Bar Crust

Vegan Hazelnut Crumb Crust

Vegan Coconut Walnut Crust

DARK CHOCOLATE CRUMB CRUST

Sometimes you just need to indulge and satisfy those chocolate cravings, and this chocolate crust will help. You can buy either chocolate crumbs in the baking aisle or a few boxes of Oreos. The Oreos have the creamy middle, which is very sweet so you can eliminate the sugar and just pulverize the cookies in a food processor. We use this crust for both the Black Forest Pie (page 203) and the Magnum P.I.e (page 209). And if you are a real chocolate lover, use this for the Triple Chocolate Cream Pie (page 189).

MAKES ONE 9-INCH PIE SHELL

½ cup (114 g) butter

2½ cups (350 g) chocolate cookie crumbs or around 30 Oreo cookies

3 Tbsp sugar (if not using Oreo cookies)

½ tsp salt

1. Preheat the oven to 350°F.

2. Melt the butter in a small saucepan or a microwave-safe dish.

3. If using the Oreo cookies, pulse them in a food processer to form a fine crumbly mixture.

4. Add the cookie crumbs, sugar, and salt into a large mixing bowl and mix to fully incorporate. Add the melted butter to the chocolate cookie crumb mixture and, using a spatula, mix thoroughly until the mixture has the consistency of wet sand and holds together when squeezed. It should also not look too greasy—if it does, add a few more crumbs.

5. Transfer the crumbs to a 9-inch pie plate. Using your hands or the bottom of a flat measuring cup or glass, push down the crumbs to neatly and evenly line the bottom and sides of the pie plate.

6. Bake for 7 minutes if you need the crust partially prebaked and 15 minutes if you need it fully blind baked. Allow the pie shell to cool completely before filling it.

CANDY BAR PIE CRUST

Currently we only use this crust for the Candy Bar Pie for Halloween. However, it really could be used for some others for that perfect mix of sweet, salty, and chocolaty goodness. The more I think about it, the more I realize we should probably use it for other pies. The To Die for Banana Cream Pie (page 171) would be amazing in this crust!

MAKES ONE 9-INCH PIE SHELL

½ cup (114 g) butter

1¼ cups (225 g) pretzels

⅔ cup (114 g) semi-sweet chocolate chips

2 Tbsp golden sugar

1. Preheat the oven to 350°F.

2. Melt the butter in a small saucepan or a microwave-safe dish.

3. In a food processor, pulse the pretzels and the chocolate chips into fine crumbs. Add the golden sugar and pulse again just enough to mix. Add the melted butter. Pulse a few more times until the mixture has the consistency of wet sand and holds together when squeezed.

4. Transfer the crumbly mixture to a 9-inch pie plate. Using your hands or the bottom of a flat measuring cup or glass, push down the crumbs to neatly and evenly line the bottom and sides of the pie plate. Dock the bottom of the dough by using a fork to prick the crust at the bottom of the plate.

5. Bake for 10 to 12 minutes, until the crust is no longer shiny. Allow the pie shell to cool completely before filling it.

NANAIMO BAR CRUST

A Nanaimo bar is made of three delicious layers. The bottom layer is, in my opinion, the best layer as it helps balance the sweetness. It also provides a great base to press when turning these classic Canadian treats into a pie!

MAKES ONE 9-INCH PIE SHELL

½ cup (114 g) butter

⅓ cup (40 g) cocoa powder

¼ cup (50 g) sugar

1 egg, beaten

1 cup (130 g) honey graham crumbs

1 cup (90 g) unsweetened shredded coconut

1. In a double boiler over medium-high heat, melt the butter with cocoa powder and sugar.

2. Temper the egg with a little bit of the melted butter mixture and then whisk into the remaining butter mixture. Cook, stirring constantly, until the mixture thickens slightly (2 to 3 minutes). Take off the heat and mix in the graham crumbs and coconut.

3. Press the mixture into your pie plate and allow to cool. No baking required! Keep the crust in the fridge while you prepare your filling.

A ll of these recipes make enough for at least one double-crust pie (one egg is enough to wash a whole lot of pies!). Which will you pick?

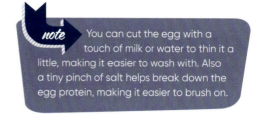
note You can cut the egg with a touch of milk or water to thin it a little, making it easier to wash with. Also a tiny pinch of salt helps break down the egg protein, making it easier to brush on.

Washes

EGG WASH

I find that a simple egg wash is the most versatile. Not only does it give that sheen and golden appearance, but it doesn't impart any real flavor, making it good for both sweet and savory pies. The fat of the egg creates the shine, and the protein provides the browning. The egg wash also protects the crust from drying out while allowing it to puff up while baking, resulting in a crisp outer layer.

1 egg

Splash of milk or water (optional)

Pinch salt (optional)

1. When ready to wash the pie, whisk the egg in a bowl until smooth and light in color. The more you whisk, the easier it is to brush on. Use a pastry brush to wash the pie per the recipe's instructions.

MILK WASH

A milk wash is great for sweet pies, as the natural sugars (the lactose) caramelize in the oven, adding a very subtle sweetness to the pastry. The top will brown nicely, but the sheen will depend on the milk fat percentage. The higher the fat, the more sheen you will get.

1 Tbsp whole milk or milk of your choice

1. When ready to wash the pie, add the milk to a small bowl. Use a pastry brush to wash the pie per the recipe's instructions.

DAIRY- & EGG-FREE WASH

If you are looking for a dairy- and egg-free alternative, there are a few options you can use. Olive oil will give the pie a golden-brown color with a little sheen. Plant-based milk or water adds moisture to help keep the crust from drying out, but neither give that golden color of egg.

1 Tbsp olive oil, plant-based milk, or water

1. When ready to wash the pie, add your wash of choice to a small bowl. Use a pastry brush to wash the pie per the recipe's instructions.

Whether you are thinking about a hearty Chicken Pot Pie (page 49) or a nice tender slow-cooked Steak & Stout Pie (page 67), there are few things more comforting than fresh-baked pie. Savory pie excites me, as I've been able to take some of my all-time favorite meals and turn them into pies. The versatility of what you can put into a flaky pie crust is really only limited by your imagination! In this chapter, I have included some classics, and some remixes that you might not be expecting.

hicken Pot Pie is probably the most classic of all the savory pies, and seriously, one that we cannot make enough of. There is something about this pie that's like a hug—it's the ultimate comfort food. If you are feeling a little under the weather, having a casual get-together, or even if it's just a cold, rainy night, this is the perfect pie.

CHICKEN POT PIE

MAKES ONE 9-INCH DOUBLE-CRUST PIE

1 recipe Double Butter Crust (page 20)

1½ lb (680 g) boneless skinless chicken thighs

2½ Tbsp vegetable oil

1 large carrot, peeled and diced

1 large onion, peeled and diced

2 stalks celery, diced

3 tsp salt

½ tsp pepper

1 Tbsp chopped fresh thyme

1 Tbsp chopped fresh sage

1½ Tbsp chopped fresh rosemary

½ tsp celery seed

¾ cup (113 g) flour

2¼ cups (560 mL) chicken stock

¾ cup (175 mL) whole milk

¾ cup frozen peas

1. Prepare a double 9-inch Double Butter Crust. Chill the dough (bottom shell in the pie plate) until you're ready to assemble your pie. Preheat the oven to 400°F. Line a baking sheet with parchment paper.

2. Spread the chicken thighs on the prepared sheet, brush them with 1 Tbsp of the oil, and sprinkle with salt and pepper. Bake for 20 to 25 minutes. Remove from the oven and let cool. Chop into bite-sized pieces.

3. In a large pot over medium-high heat, heat the remaining oil for 30 to 45 seconds, then add the carrots, onions, and celery. Stir the vegetables to coat and cook for 7 to 10 minutes, until the onions are translucent. Add the salt, pepper, thyme, sage, rosemary (reserve ½ Tbsp for garnish), and celery seed. Stir well and cook for 1 minute.

4. Sprinkle the flour over the vegetables and stir to coat evenly. Cook, stirring, for another 2 minutes. Add the chicken stock and the milk, mix well, and reduce the temperature to medium-low. Continue to cook until the mixture begins to thicken, stirring frequently to keep it from sticking to the bottom of the pot, then remove from the heat.

5. Add the chopped chicken and the peas to the filling, and allow to cool completely to room temperature. *Tip: You can make the pie up to this step the day before, if you keep the filling in the fridge.*

6. Add the filling to the bottom pie shell and smooth it out to have a nice even top. Follow the steps for adding the top crust (page 24) and sprinkle with the remaining rosemary. Cut four 1-inch slits in the top of the pie. Chill for 30 minutes in the fridge or 15 minutes in the freezer before baking.

7. Preheat the oven to 350°F. Line a baking sheet with parchment paper. Transfer the pie to the prepared baking sheet.

8. Bake for 60 to 70 minutes, until the top is golden brown. Some of the filling may start to bubble out of the vent holes. Let cool for 10 to 15 minutes before serving, as it will be extremely hot.

his one is my husband's favorite savory pie. What is not to love about roasted chicken in a creamy Alfredo sauce with bacon, onions, peas, and lots of cheese?

CHICKEN CARBONARA PIE

MAKES ONE 9-INCH DOUBLE-CRUST PIE

1 recipe Double Butter Crust (page 20)

1½ lb (680 g) boneless skinless chicken thighs or breasts

1 Tbsp olive oil

½ cup (114 g) butter

1 large clove garlic, minced

2 Tbsp flour

2½ cups (625 mL) heavy cream

½ cup (65 g) grated parmesan cheese

¾ cup (75 g) grated mozzarella

½ tsp fresh ground pepper

1¼ tsp salt

Pinch white pepper

1 medium onion, peeled and diced

1 cup fresh or frozen peas

4 slices bacon, cooked and crumbled

note We use chicken thighs because they tend to have more flavor and be more tender.

1. Prepare a double 9-inch Double Butter Crust. Chill the dough (bottom shell in the pie plate) until ready to assemble your pie. Preheat the oven to 400°F. Line a baking sheet with parchment paper.

2. Spread the chicken thighs on the prepared sheet, then brush them with the olive oil and sprinkle with salt and pepper. Bake for 20 to 25 minutes. Remove from the oven and let cool. The chicken should be fully cooked at this point, but don't worry if it is not quite done, as it will bake in the pie for another hour or more.

3. In a large pot over medium heat, heat the butter and garlic, stirring constantly. Once the butter has fully melted, stir in the flour to form a thick paste and cook for 30 to 60 seconds. Add the cream slowly, while whisking quickly, to avoid any lumps. Cook until the mixture thickens. Add the parmesan (reserve 1 tsp to top the pie) and mozzarella to the pot, stir, and remove from the heat. Continue to stir until all the cheese has melted. Add the pepper, salt, and white pepper and mix well.

4. Cut the chicken into bite-sized pieces. Add it to the Alfredo sauce along with the onions, peas, and cooked bacon, mixing well to combine. Allow the filling to cool completely to room temperature. *Tip: You can make the pie up to this step the day before, if you keep the filling in the fridge.*

5. Pour the chicken carbonara mixture into the bottom pie shell and smooth it out to have a nice even top. Follow the steps for adding the top crust (page 24) and sprinkle with the remaining parmesan cheese. Cut four 1-inch slits in the top of the pie. Chill for 30 minutes in the fridge or 15 minutes in the freezer before baking.

6. Preheat the oven to 350°F. Line a baking sheet with parchment paper. Transfer the pie to the other prepared baking sheet.

7. Bake for 60 to 70 minutes, until the top is golden brown. Some of the filling may start to bubble out of the vent holes. Let cool for 10 to 15 minutes before serving, as it will be extremely hot.

A sweet, creamy coconut curry–inspired Thai chicken pie. With sweet bell peppers, Thai basil, and chicken, this is a uniquely delicious take on a chicken pie.

THAI CHICKEN PIE

MAKES ONE 9-INCH DOUBLE-CRUST PIE

1 recipe Double Butter Crust (page 20)

1½ lb (680 g) boneless skinless chicken thighs

3 Tbsp oil

1 tsp salt

½ tsp pepper

4 Tbsp curry powder

1 tsp garlic powder

½ small red onion, peeled and diced

1 small red bell pepper, diced

1 small yellow bell pepper, diced

1 Thai chili pepper, finely diced

1 tsp finely diced lemongrass (white part only)

1 tsp peeled and grated ginger

⅓ cup (50 g) flour

2 cups (500 mL) coconut milk

1 tsp red curry paste

½ tsp Sriracha hot sauce

2 Tbsp chopped Thai basil

1. Prepare a double 9-inch Double Butter Crust. Chill the dough (bottom shell in the pie plate) until ready to assemble your pie. Preheat the oven to 400°F. Line a baking sheet with parchment paper.

2. In a mixing bowl, add the chicken, 1 Tbsp of the oil, and the salt, pepper, curry powder, and garlic powder. Mix to evenly coat and marinate for a minimum of 30 minutes. Spread the chicken thighs onto the prepared sheet and bake for 20 to 25 minutes. Remove from the oven and let cool. The chicken should be fully cooked at this point, but do not worry if it is not, as it will bake in the pie for another 60 to 70 minutes. Cut into bite-sized pieces.

3. In a large pot over medium-high heat, heat the remaining oil. Add the red onions, red peppers, yellow peppers, Thai chilies, lemongrass, and ginger. Cook until the vegetables just start to soften, 6 to 8 minutes, stirring frequently. Add the flour and stir well to evenly coat the veggies. Add the coconut milk and mix well, then stir in the red curry paste and hot sauce. Continue to stir until the mixture thickens. Remove from the heat. Add the chicken pieces and basil and mix thoroughly. Let cool completely.

Tip: *You can make the pie up to this step the day before, if you keep the filling in the fridge.*

4. Add the Thai chicken mixture to the bottom pie shell and smooth it out to have a nice even top. Follow the steps for adding the top crust (page 24). Cut four 1-inch slits in the top of the pie. Chill for 30 minutes in the fridge or 15 minutes in the freezer before baking.

5. Preheat the oven to 350°F. Line a baking sheet with parchment paper. Transfer the pie to the prepared baking sheet.

6. Bake for 60 to 70 minutes, until the top is golden brown. Some of the filling may start to bubble out of the vent holes. Let cool for 10 to 15 minutes before serving, as it will be extremely hot.

aribbean cuisine has lots of different influences. For our Caribbean-inspired chicken pie, instead of going the predictable jerk flavor route, we decided to develop a more complex Caribbean curry with lots of veggies and spices and, of course, some heat.

CARIBBEAN CHICKEN PIE

MAKES ONE 9-INCH DOUBLE-CRUST PIE

1 recipe Double Butter Crust (page 20)

1 lb (454 g) boneless skinless chicken thighs

1 medium carrot, peeled and diced, peels reserved

1 small yellow onion, peeled and diced, peels reserved

1 tsp peeled grated ginger, peels reserved

1 stalk celery, finely diced, trim reserved

1 russet potato, peeled and diced

1 Tbsp butter

1 clove garlic, peeled and minced

1 Scotch bonnet pepper, finely diced

1 tsp curry powder

¼ cup chopped green onions

1 tsp dried thyme

Pinch ground sage

1 tsp salt

1½ cups (375 mL) reserved stock

½ cup (125 mL) coconut milk

½ tsp soy sauce

⅓ cup (50 g) flour

½ cup fresh or frozen peas

1 Tbsp cilantro, finely chopped

¼ tsp ground turmeric (optional)

1. Prepare a double 9-inch Double Butter Crust. Chill the dough (bottom shell in the pie plate) until you're ready to assemble your pie. Preheat the oven to 400°F. Line a baking sheet with parchment paper.

2. In a large Dutch oven, cover the chicken thighs with water. Add the trim from the carrot, onion, ginger, and celery. Cook until the chicken is falling apart, about 90 minutes. Remove the chicken and shred with a couple of forks. Strain the stock and reserve.

3. Over high heat, bring a medium pot of salted water to a boil. Add the carrots and potatoes and cook for 8 to 10 minutes until just tender.

4. In the Dutch oven over medium-high heat, sauté the butter, garlic, celery, onions, ginger, Scotch bonnet peppers, and curry powder for 5 to 7 minutes, until the onions are translucent. Add the carrots and potatoes and the shredded chicken, green onions, thyme, sage, and salt. Sauté for another 2 to 4 minutes.

5. In a small bowl, whisk the stock, coconut milk, soy sauce, and flour until smooth. Add to the chicken mixture and continue to stir until thickened, 7 to 10 minutes. Add the peas and cilantro. Remove from the heat and allow to cool completely to room temperature. *Tip: You can make the pie up to this step the day before, if you keep the filling in the fridge.*

6. Add the chicken mixture to the bottom pie shell and smooth it out to have a nice even top. Follow the steps for adding the top crust (page 24). Whisk the turmeric into the egg wash, and brush the wash onto the whole surface of the pie. Cut four 1-inch slits to vent the pie. Chill for 30 minutes in the fridge or 15 minutes in the freezer before baking.

7. Preheat the oven to 350°F. Transfer the pie to the prepared baking sheet.

8. Bake for 60 to 70 minutes, until the top is golden brown. Some of the filling may start to bubble out of the vent holes. Let cool for 10 to 15 minutes before serving, as it will be extremely hot.

note You can substitute the Scotch bonnet pepper for 1 habanero pepper or 1 tsp of Scotch bonnet hot sauce.

L iving in Vancouver, so close to the ocean, we are fortunate to have access to some of the freshest seafood. In this pie, a nice thick, creamy salmon chowder with corn and fresh herbs pairs perfectly with the flaky Double Butter Crust.

SALMON BACON CHOWDER PIE

MAKES ONE 9-INCH DOUBLE-CRUST PIE

1 recipe Double Butter Crust (page 20)

1 Tbsp butter

4 slices bacon, raw and chopped

1 medium onion, peeled and diced

½ cup frozen or fresh corn

2 cloves garlic, peeled and minced

1 Tbsp chopped thyme

1 bay leaf

¼ tsp chili flakes

1 large red potato, diced

⅓ cup (50 g) flour

2 cups (500 mL) milk

½ cup (125 mL) heavy cream

1 lb (454 g) wild salmon fillet, skin removed and deboned, and cut into ½-inch pieces

2 Tbsp lemon juice

1 tsp salt

½ tsp pepper

1. Prepare a double 9-inch Double Butter Crust. Chill the dough (bottom shell in the pie plate) until you're ready to assemble your pie. Line a baking sheet with parchment paper.

2. In a large pot over medium heat, heat the butter. Add the bacon and cook for 2 to 3 minutes. Add the onions, corn, garlic, thyme, bay leaf, and chili flakes and cook for 7 to 10 minutes, until the onions are translucent.

3. Bring a separate pot of salted water to a boil and cook the potatoes just until tender, 8 to 10 minutes, being careful not to overcook. Drain and set aside.

4. Add the flour to the onion mixture and stir to coat evenly. Cook, stirring constantly, for 1 to 2 minutes, then stir in the milk and cream and cook until the mixture thickens. Add the salmon, lemon juice, salt, and pepper. The heat from the chowder will cook the salmon. Remove from the heat and allow to cool completely.

5. Add the salmon chowder mixture to the bottom pie shell and smooth it out to have a nice even top. Follow the steps for adding the top crust (page 24). Cut four 1-inch slits to vent the pie. Chill for 30 minutes in the fridge or 15 minutes in the freezer before baking.

6. Preheat the oven to 350°F. Transfer the pie to the prepared baking sheet.

7. Bake for 60 to 70 minutes, until the top is golden brown. Some of the filling may start to bubble out of the vent holes. Let cool for 10 to 15 minutes before serving, as it will be extremely hot.

f all the savory pies I've developed, this one took the longest. It was so important to get the taste and feeling of a cheeseburger in every bite. And it was worth it—this has become one of our top-selling savory pies. There's a subtle hint of crunchy dill pickle, smoky crumbled bacon, a squeeze of mustard, lots of sharp cheddar cheese . . . and let's not forget the flaky pie crust (adorned with sesame seeds, of course, so you don't miss the bun)!

BACON CHEESEBURGER PIE

MAKES ONE 9-INCH DOUBLE-CRUST PIE (OR FOUR 5-INCH DOUBLE-CRUST PIES AS SHOWN IN PHOTO)

1 recipe Double Butter Crust (page 20)

1½ lb (680 g) ground beef

½ cup (75 g) flour

3 cups (750 mL) milk

2 Tbsp mustard, plus additional for topping (optional)

1 Tbsp salt

½ tsp white pepper

2 cups (200 g) grated cheddar cheese

2 dill pickles, coarsely diced

6 slices bacon, cooked and crumbled

¼ cup finely diced onions (optional)

1 tsp sesame seeds

1. Prepare a double 9-inch or four 5-inch Double Butter Crust(s). Chill the dough (bottom shell(s) in the pie plate(s)) until you're ready to assemble your pie. Line a baking sheet with parchment paper.

2. In a large skillet over medium-high heat, brown the beef, breaking apart any large clumps. Drain off some of the fat by pouring the cooked beef into a colander. You do not have to be too methodical about shaking the colander, and definitely don't rinse the beef. If a little fat is left, that is flavor—this is a burger, after all!

3. Sprinkle the flour over the beef and mix it in to coat the meat evenly. It will disappear as it absorbs the beef drippings. Cook for 1 to 2 minutes. Slowly add the milk, continuing to stir. We are building the béchamel sauce right into the beef! Add the mustard, salt, and white pepper and give it another good stir, then stir in half the grated cheddar cheese and remove from the heat. Keep stirring until the cheese is completely melted, then fold in the pickles. Allow the filling to cool completely to room temperature, or chill in the refrigerator. *Tip:* You can make the pie up to this step the day before, if you keep the filling in the fridge.

4. Add the beef mixture to the bottom pie shell and smooth it out to have a nice even top. Top with the remaining cheddar cheese, a swirl of mustard just as you would top your burger (use as much or little as you like, depending on how much you love/hate mustard on a burger), crumbled bacon, and onions. Follow the steps for adding the top crust (page 24), and sprinkle with sesame seeds. Cut four 1-inch slits to vent the pie. Chill for 30 minutes in the fridge or 15 minutes in the freezer before baking.

5. Preheat the oven to 350°F. Transfer the pie to the prepared sheet.

6. Bake for 60 to 70 minutes, until the top is golden brown. Some of the filling may start to bubble out of the vent holes. Let cool for 10 to 15 minutes before serving, as it will be extremely hot.

hen I first started The Pie Hole, I tried really hard to get out of the bakery in time to catch the Vancouver Canucks hockey games. Game night was a big part of my life—I worked so hard, and it gave me some much-needed time to spend with friends. At the time, the Sedin twins were the stars on the team. When they announced their retirement, I decided that I wanted to create a Swedish-inspired pie and donate all the proceeds to the Canucks for Kids Fund, an organization that meant a lot to these two players. This pie is my small tribute to them.

SWEDISH MEATBALL PIE

MAKES ONE 9-INCH SINGLE-CRUST PIE

½ recipe Double Butter Crust (page 20)

Meatballs

1¼ cups (63 g) fresh breadcrumbs

½ cup (125 mL) heavy cream

5 Tbsp (70 g) butter

½ large onion, finely diced

13 oz (375 g) ground beef

7 oz (200 g) ground pork

2 eggs

½ Tbsp golden sugar

1 tsp salt

½ tsp pepper

1 tsp nutmeg

½ tsp allspice

Pinch ground ginger

1½ Tbsp finely chopped parsley

1 cup (250 mL) chicken broth

1. Prepare a single 9-inch Double Butter Crust and partially blind bake (page 24). Chill the dough in the pie plate until you're ready to assemble your pie. Line a baking sheet with parchment paper. Preheat the oven to 350°F.

2. Place the breadcrumbs in a large mixing bowl. Gently stir in the cream, cover, and let sit for 10 minutes.

3. While the breadcrumbs are soaking, in a large pan over medium heat, melt 1 Tbsp of the butter. Add the onions and cook, stirring frequently, until they are translucent and just starting to brown, 7 to 10 minutes. Remove the onions to a large bowl. Add the ground beef, pork, eggs, golden sugar, salt, pepper, nutmeg, allspice, and ginger, and mix well. Add the breadcrumb mixture and the chopped parsley and mix gently with clean hands until all the ingredients are fully incorporated. Shape the mixture into 2-inch meatballs. You will need about 15 to fill the pie.

4. In a large skillet over medium-high heat, melt the remaining butter. Add all the meatballs, unless your skillet is not large enough, in which case you may have to do 2 batches. Cook the meatballs until the outsides are browned.

5. Transfer the meatballs to a medium-sized baking pan and pour in the chicken broth. There's no need to wash the skillet—you'll use it again. Cover the pan with foil and bake for 40 minutes. Remove from the oven and let cool completely before assembling the pie.

Gravy

1½ cups (375 mL) beef broth

¼ cup (38 g) flour

Salt

Pepper

Cabbage

1 Tbsp butter

1 medium red onion, finely diced

½ Granny Smith apple, peeled
   and shredded

2 cups thinly sliced red cabbage

⅓ cup (80 mL) red cooking wine

1 Tbsp apple cider vinegar

¼ cup (50 g) golden sugar

1 tsp caraway seeds

¼ tsp allspice

¼ tsp salt

Pinch pepper

Brown Buttered Dill Potatoes

4 cups diced white potatoes
   (½–inch pieces), skins on
   (3–4 potatoes)

⅓ cup (76 g) butter

1 Tbsp finely chopped dill

½ tsp salt

¼ tsp pepper

6. For the gravy, in the skillet used for browning the meatballs, heat ¼ cup of the beef broth over medium-high heat to deglaze the pan, stirring and lifting up all the bits of flavor left from the meatballs. Add the flour and stir to make a paste. Add the rest of the beef broth and whisk until the mixture is nice and smooth. Cook until the sauce thickens, then season to taste with salt and pepper. Set the gravy aside to cool in preparation for pie assembly.

7. For the cabbage, in a large clean skillet over medium-high heat, melt the butter and sauté the onions for a few minutes, until they begin to sweat. Add the shredded apple and reduce the heat to medium. Cook for a few more minutes, stirring frequently. Add the cabbage. Give it a good stir and cover the skillet to allow the steam to help cook the cabbage for 7 to 10 minutes.

8. Add the wine, vinegar, golden sugar, caraway seeds, allspice, salt, and pepper. Cook, uncovered, for another 10 to 12 minutes to reduce the added fluids until the mixture is no longer wet. Transfer the mixture to a container and let cool completely.

9. For the potatoes, bring a large pot of salted water to a boil, then add the potatoes and cook for about 12 minutes or until they are tender but not falling apart, and you can easily pierce them with a fork. Remove the potatoes from the heat, drain, and transfer to a medium-sized bowl.

10. In a small saucepan over medium-high heat, begin to melt the butter. To make brown butter, continue to cook until the butter starts to foam and turns brown. You can swirl the pot, but there's no need to stir. It is done when you smell a lovely nutty aroma.

11. Pour the brown butter over the potatoes, then add the dill, salt, and pepper. Gently toss to evenly coat the potatoes, then set aside to cool.

12. Preheat the oven to 350°F.

13. To assemble the pie, combine the chilled meatballs and gravy in a large bowl and toss to coat. Line the bottom of the pie shell with the mixture, making sure the meatballs are close together in a single layer. Every slice should get lots of meatball. Top with the cabbage and then the potatoes.

14. Bake for 40 to 45 minutes, until the potatoes are crispy. Remove from the oven and wait 5 to 10 minutes before serving, as it will be extremely hot!

his traditional French stew in a pie features a hearty, delicious filling of beef, root vegetables, and fresh herbs braised in red wine and cognac. This comforting dinner pie will have you saying, *oh là là!*

BEEF BOURGUIGNON PIE

MAKES ONE 9-INCH DOUBLE-CRUST PIE

1 recipe Double Butter Crust (page 20)

2 Tbsp oil

1 carrot, peeled and diced

1 onion, peeled and diced

½ cup peeled and diced rutabagas

1 parsnip, peeled and diced parsnips

2 Tbsp finely chopped thyme

14 oz (400 g) stewing beef, cut into ½-inch pieces

1 cup (250 mL) red wine

2 Tbsp cognac

2½ cups (625 mL) beef stock

1 Tbsp Worcestershire sauce

1 Tbsp tomato paste

1 tsp salt

1 tsp pepper, plus more for sprinkling

1 cup sliced mushrooms

3 slices bacon, cooked and crumbled

¼ cup (38 g) flour

1 cup (250 mL) water

1. Prepare a double 9-inch Double Butter Crust. Chill the dough (bottom shell in the pie plate) until you're ready to assemble your pie. Line a baking sheet with parchment paper.

2. In a large pot over medium-high heat, heat the oil. Add the carrots, onions, rutabagas, parsnips, and thyme (reserve a pinch to finish the top crust of the pie later). Cook for about 7 minutes, stirring frequently, until the onions are translucent then remove the vegetables and set aside. Add the beef and cook until the beef has browned on all sides, 3 to 4 minutes. Don't worry if the bottom of the pot gets dark; it will add to the flavor. Add the wine and brandy and stir to deglaze the bottom of the pot. Add the beef stock, Worcestershire sauce, tomato paste, salt, and pepper. Mix well. Return the reserved vegetables to the pot. Reduce the heat to low, cover, and simmer for 2 hours, stirring occasionally. Once the beef is falling-apart tender, add the mushrooms and bacon, stirring frequently, and cook until the mushrooms soften.

3. In a large bowl, combine the flour and the water. Whisk until the mixture is smooth and pourable, adding small amounts of water to thin out if needed. Pour into the beef bourguignon and stir. As the flour cooks, it will thicken the mixture. If after 5 to 7 minutes the mixture is not thick enough, repeat with additional flour, a tablespoon at a time, to achieve a thick, gravy-like consistency. It will thicken as it cools as well. Cool to room temperature.

4. Add the beef mixture to the bottom pie shell and smooth it out to make a nice even top. Follow the steps for adding the top crust (page 24). Cut four 1-inch slits to vent the pie. Chill for 30 minutes in the fridge or 15 minutes in the freezer before baking.

5. Preheat the oven to 350°F. Transfer the pie to the prepared baking sheet.

6. Bake for 60 to 70 minutes, until the top is golden brown. Some of the filling may start to bubble out the vent holes. Let cool for 10 to 15 minutes before serving, as it will be extremely hot.

This recipe has been on our menu since day one. The beef is slowly cooked in a dark stout beer (we have a lot of great breweries nearby, so we go local) until it is falling-apart tender. The rich stout gravy with our buttery crust is the perfect combination . . . so this recipe is going nowhere.

STEAK & STOUT PIE

MAKES ONE 9-INCH DOUBLE-CRUST PIE

1 recipe Double Butter Crust (page 20)

2 Tbsp oil

1 large onion, peeled and diced

2 carrots, peeled and diced

1½ lb (680 g) stewing beef, cut into ½-inch pieces

Two 15 oz (425 mL) cans stout beer

2 cups (500 mL) beef stock

1 Tbsp Worcestershire sauce

2 Tbsp tomato paste

2 tsp salt

1 tsp pepper

½ cup (75 g) flour

1 cup (250 mL) water

1. Prepare a double 9-inch Double Butter Crust. Chill the dough (bottom shell in the pie plate) until you're ready to assemble your pie. Line a baking sheet with parchment paper.

2. In a large pot over medium heat, heat the oil. Add the onions and carrots and cook for 7 minutes, stirring frequently, until the onions are translucent. Remove and set aside. Add in the beef and cook until it is brown on all sides. Add the beer, beef stock, Worcestershire sauce, and tomato paste and mix well. Add the salt and pepper and the reserved vegetables back to the pot. Simmer over low heat for at least 3 hours, stirring frequently, until the beef is very tender and falls apart if you push a piece against the side of the pot.

3. In a bowl, combine the flour with the water and whisk until smooth and lump free. Stir into the steak and stout mixture and cook to thicken, 10 to 15 minutes. If it isn't thick enough, make a little more flour and water mixture to thicken. Once the mixture has reached the consistency of gravy, taste and add more salt and pepper if needed. Allow the filling to cool completely to room temperature or chill in the refrigerator. You can make the pie up until this point the day before.

4. Add the beef mixture to the bottom pie shell and smooth it out to make a nice even top. Follow the steps for adding the top crust (page 24), and sprinkle with pepper. Cut four 1-inch slits to vent the pie. Chill for 30 minutes in the fridge or 15 minutes in the freezer before baking.

5. Preheat the oven to 350°F. Transfer the pie to the prepared baking sheet.

6. Bake for 60 to 70 minutes, until the top is golden brown. Some of the filling may start to bubble out the vent holes. Let cool for 10 to 15 minutes before serving, as it will be extremely hot.

ur Shepherd's Pie is actually a mixture between Shepherd's Pie and Cottage Pie, with a blend of lamb and beef slow cooked down with vegetables and gravy, and topped with buttery, fluffy mashed potatoes. With the addition of the pie shell, I guess we should call it a Shepherd's Pie Pie.

SHEPHERD'S PIE

MAKES ONE 9-INCH SINGLE-CRUST PIE

½ recipe Double Butter Crust (page 20)

2 Tbsp oil

1½ cups peeled and diced carrots

1 cup peeled and diced onions

1½ lb (680 g) ground lamb

¾ lb (340 g) ground beef

3 Tbsp tomato paste

2 Tbsp Worcestershire sauce

2 cloves garlic, peeled and minced

1 tsp rosemary

Pinch thyme

3 tsp salt

½ tsp black pepper

¼ cup (38 g) flour

½ cup (125 mL) chicken stock

1 cup frozen corn

1 cup frozen peas

5 large russet potatoes, peeled and quartered

⅔ cup (150 mL) milk

6 Tbsp (85 g) butter

½ tsp white pepper

Pinch paprika

Parsley, chopped, for garnish

1. Prepare a single 9-inch Double Butter Crust and partially blind bake (page 24). Chill the dough in the pie plate until you're ready to assemble your pie. Line a baking sheet with parchment paper.

2. In a large pot over medium-high heat, heat the oil. Add the carrots and onions and cook for 7 minutes, until they just start to sweat. They should still be a bit firm. Remove from pot and set aside.

3. In the same pot, over medium-high heat, combine the lamb and beef. Cook, breaking apart any large chunks with a spoon, until the meat is three-quarters brown, about 10 minutes. Drain some of the fat from the pan. Add the tomato paste, Worcestershire sauce, garlic, rosemary, thyme, 2 tsp of the salt, and the black pepper. Mix well to fully incorporate. Once fully cooked, add the carrots and onions and cook, stirring, for 5 minutes.

4. Sprinkle the flour over the mixture and stir it in. Add the chicken stock, corn, and peas, and cook until the mixture thickens up. Add more salt and pepper if needed, then remove from the heat.

5. In a large pot of salted water, bring the potatoes to a boil over high heat, and boil for 20 minutes, until easy to pierce with a fork. Drain and return to the pot. Reduce the heat to low for 1 minute to steam off any excess water, then remove from the heat.

6. Add the milk, butter, remaining salt, and the white pepper to the potatoes. Use a hand masher or your stand mixer to whip the potatoes until they are nice and fluffy.

7. Preheat the oven to 350°F. Fill the blind-baked pie shell with the meat filling, and top with the mashed potatoes, spreading them right to the edge of the crust to seal in the goodness. Sprinkle with paprika. Transfer the pie to the prepared baking sheet.

8. Bake for 35 to 40 minutes, until the potatoes are golden on top. Garnish with parsley.

Tourtière is a very traditional French Canadian dish. I have actually never spent any time in that region of Canada; I was born and raised on the West Coast. But when you own a pie company in Canada, you have to learn all about it! People who grew up with this pie are very particular about their tourtière, and the ingredients vary depending on where in Quebec you grew up and what your family's recipe was. Our Pie Hole version has received rave reviews from many of our French Canadian customers. Not bad for a West Coast girl!

TOURTIÈRE PIE

MAKES ONE 9-INCH DOUBLE-CRUST PIE

1 recipe Double Butter Crust (page 20)

1½ lb (680 g) lean ground pork

¾ lb (340 g) lean ground beef

2 medium onions, peeled and diced

2½ cups (625 mL) water

2 cloves garlic, peeled and minced

1½ tsp salt

1½ tsp ground thyme

1 tsp ground sage

½ tsp pepper

¼ tsp cinnamon

¼ tsp ground cloves

1. Prepare a double 9-inch Double Butter Crust. Chill (bottom shell in the pie plate) until you're ready to assemble your pie. Line a baking sheet with parchment paper.

2. In a large pot over medium-high heat, brown the pork, beef, and onions. Drain the mixture quickly, getting rid of 90% of the fat (but not all of it, as it adds flavor). Add the water, garlic, salt, thyme, sage, pepper, cinnamon, and cloves and reduce the heat to medium-low. Simmer for 35 to 40 minutes, stirring occasionally, until the fluid has reduced by 75%.

3. Let the mixture cool a little and break down the meat, either in your food processor (working in small batches) or with an immersion blender until it is fine, but not pâté. Allow the mixture to cool completely before filling the pie.

4. Add the tourtière mixture to the bottom pie shell and smooth it out to make a nice even top. Follow the steps for adding the top crust (page 24). Cut four 1-inch slits to vent the pie. I like to decorate this pie with little cut-out pastry leaves or a fleur-de-lis for that true Quebecois feel. Chill for 30 minutes in the fridge or 15 minutes in the freezer before baking.

5. Preheat the oven to 350°F. Transfer the pie to the prepared baking sheet.

6. Bake for 60 to 70 minutes, until the top is golden brown. Some of the filling may start to bubble out the vent holes. Let cool for 10 to 15 minutes before serving, as it will be extremely hot.

PIE
MEMORIES

IN MY EARLY DAYS OF SLINGING PIES,
back before I had my shops, I was popping up at
different farmers' markets and food truck festivals.
One unique venue I found was a place known to
Vancouver hipsters as the "Yellow House." It was
a beautiful old character house in East Vancouver
where a collective known as "the Association of
Very Good Ideas" hosted various events. One
of these was a yearly pie competition, where pie
makers could bring several pies to share with
paying ticket holders, who would vote for their
favorites in multiple categories.

I participated in the Incredible Pie Competition
only once, but it was an unforgettable experience.
The pie I entered was a new addition to my
growing menu, a Pulled Pork Pie (page 74).
Pulled pork was the super-trendy ingredient at
the time. It was showing up in so many recipes,
so why not in a pie? I smoked a nice pork shoulder, slow roasted it until it was falling apart, and
combined it with a smoky sweet barbecue sauce,
bourbon baked beans, and bacon, all topped with
sweet, buttery golden cornbread.

So many people showed up that afternoon
to eat pie. It was a great deal—only $5 for a
wristband that allowed you to try a few dozen
different pies! I met so many pie-loving fanatics
that I realized that the people of Vancouver not
only needed a pie bakery, but really wanted one.
Their support was incredible, and their excitement
about trying my pie was so genuine. After an
afternoon in the sun, the votes were tallied and
the organizers started to announce the winners.
The crowd of nearly 200 people gathered on the
lawn, cross-legged, applauding and cheering
loudly as the winners for Best Sweet, Best Vegan,
and Best Sculptural pies were announced, and the
winners proudly went to accept their ribbons.

There was a winner's wheel covered with
what I had assumed were prizes, but upon closer
inspection, they were anything but. This was my
worst nightmare. What if I won? I would have
to spin the wheel. What if the wheel landed on
"Five Minutes of Interpretive Dance"? (Yes, that
was on there!) When my category, Best Savory,
came up, I wasn't sure I wanted to win and
spin that wheel, but my name was called over
a bullhorn. I nervously walked through a sea
of people, carefully stepping over crossed limbs.
The crowd started slowly chanting "pulled pork,
pulled pork, pulled pork."

As I reached the front, a handcrafted sparkly
glitter ribbon was pinned to my shirt and I was
directed to spin the wheel. With fingers and
toes crossed, I spun the wheel and prayed that I
wouldn't have to make up and perform a rap song
in front of a group of strangers. Tick, tick, tick,
tick . . . the spinning wheel started to slow, finally
landing on "Give Out 10 High Fives," the least
embarrassing thing up there. I was so relieved.
As I made my way out of the crowd, I high-fived
everyone I passed. Over the years I have told
this story many times, and reflecting on it, I am
so proud I had my "pulled pork" moment.

ulled pork came on the scene about a decade ago in a really big way. It was always around, but suddenly, it was everywhere. So why not in a pie? What really sets ours apart from other recipes is the very unconventional topping of golden cornbread.

PULLED PORK PIE

MAKES ONE 9-INCH SINGLE-CRUST PIE

½ recipe Double Butter Crust (page 20)

Pork

2 tsp chili powder

2 tsp cumin

1 tsp garlic powder

1 tsp mustard powder

2 tsp salt

1 tsp pepper

1 tsp smoked paprika

½ tsp cayenne pepper

6 cloves garlic, peeled and minced

2 lb (910 g) boneless pork shoulder

4 cups (1 L) water

Barbecue Sauce

1 Tbsp butter

1 onion, finely diced

1 cup (250 mL) ketchup

¼ cup (60 mL) lemon juice

⅓ cup (66 g) golden sugar

1 Tbsp Worcestershire sauce

2 tsp mustard

1 tsp salt

1 tsp chili powder

½ tsp pepper

2 Tbsp bourbon

1. Prepare a single 9-inch Double Butter Crust and fully blind bake (page 24). Chill the dough (bottom shell in the pie plate) until you're ready to assemble your pie. Preheat the oven to 450°F.

2. For the pork, in a small bowl, mix the chili powder, cumin, garlic powder, mustard powder, salt, pepper, paprika, and cayenne, then massage them into the pork, covering it completely. Place the pork shoulder in a roasting pan (or use a slow cooker to simmer all day until the meat is falling apart). Distribute the garlic over the meat and add the water. Cover the pan with foil.

3. Roast for 30 minutes, then reduce the heat to 300°F and cook for at least 2 hours, until the pork pulls apart with a fork. Let the pork cool slightly, then pull apart with 2 forks. This is easiest when it is still a little warm.

4. For the barbecue sauce, in a small saucepan over medium-high heat, melt the butter. Add the onions and cook for 5 to 7 minutes until translucent and soft. Add the ketchup, lemon juice, golden sugar, Worcestershire sauce, mustard, salt, chili powder, and pepper, and reduce the heat to low. Simmer for 15 to 20 minutes, stirring in the bourbon in the last 5 minutes.

5. Remove from the heat and pour the sauce over the pulled pork, mixing well to evenly coat the meat. Allow to cool.

6. For the baked beans, in a large saucepan over medium-high heat, bring the beans, onions, molasses, coffee, garlic powder, and chili flakes to a simmer. Reduce the heat to low and simmer for about 40 minutes, stirring frequently. Add the bacon and bourbon, stir well, and cook for an additional 5 to 7 minutes. Remove from the heat and cool.

7. Preheat the oven to 350°F.

8. For the cornbread topping, in a large bowl, combine the flour, sugar, cornmeal, baking powder, and salt. Mix well to combine. Add the milk, egg, oil, butter, and honey and whisk until nice and smooth. Set aside for assembly.

Baked Beans

One 14 oz (398 g) can beans in tomato sauce

1 onion, peeled and diced

¼ cup (60 mL) fancy molasses

1 Tbsp instant coffee

1 tsp garlic powder

½ tsp chili flakes

5 slices cooked bacon, crumbled

1 Tbsp bourbon

Cornbread Topping

¾ cup (113 g) flour

⅓ cup (66 g) sugar

¼ cup (45 g) cornmeal

½ Tbsp baking powder

¼ tsp salt

⅔ cup (150 mL) milk

1 egg, beaten

3 Tbsp oil

1 Tbsp butter, melted

½ Tbsp honey

9. To assemble the pie, add the pulled pork to the pie shell, filling it about half full. Top with the bourbon baked beans leaving room to pour the cornbread batter overtop.

10. Preheat the oven to 350°F. Transfer the pie to the prepared baking sheet.

11. Bake for 35 to 40 minutes, until the topping is golden brown and set in the middle (with a little spring back if lightly touched). Let cool for 10 to 15 minutes before serving, as it will be extremely hot.

note Cornbread batter doesn't hold up well. Once added to the top of the pie it should be baked right away. If you have too much, pour the extra batter into a greased muffin tin to make some delicious cornbread muffins. Bake them for 15 to 17 minutes at 350°F.

ometimes, after a really good meal, I want to create a pie version of the food I just ate. That's how this pie happened. One of my favorite taco spots does a killer Korean pork taco, so I went to a Korean market and picked up all the ingredients. That alone was inspiring—there are so many cool things in it. I truly believe you can put just about anything in a pie crust!

KOREAN PORK HANDPIES

MAKES 8 HANDPIES

½ recipe Double Butter Crust (page 20)

1 lb (454 g) pork loin

1 cup (200 g) golden sugar

2 Tbsp peeled and grated ginger

½ cup + 2 Tbsp (150 mL) soy sauce

½ cup (60 mL) gochujang sauce (mild/medium)

3 Tbsp sesame oil

2 cloves garlic, peeled and minced

2 tsp ground ginger

¾ cup chopped green onions

½ cup shredded green napa cabbage

½ cup shredded red cabbage

¾ cup peeled and shredded daikon

½ cup peeled and shredded jicama

½ cup peeled and julienned carrots

¼ cup peeled and thinly sliced onions

⅔ cup (150 mL) mayonnaise

2 Tbsp rice vinegar

Egg Wash (page 43)

2 Tbsp black sesame seeds

1. Prepare a single Double Butter Crust, and cut into eight 7-inch rounds. Chill the dough until you're ready to assemble your handpies. Line a baking sheet with parchment paper.

2. In a slow cooker or roasting pan, place the pork loin and add just enough water to cover it. Add ¼ cup of the golden sugar, the ginger, and 2 Tbsp of the soy sauce. Cover and simmer for 3 to 4 hours on high in a slow cooker, or covered in a Dutch oven or roasting pan with foil for 2 hours, or until it's easy to pull apart with a fork. Drain all the liquid and shred the pork using 2 forks while it is still hot.

3. In a bowl, combine the rest of the golden sugar, the remaining soy sauce, gochujang, sesame oil, garlic, ginger, and ¼ cup of the green onions. Mix very well, then pour the sauce over the shredded pork and stir to evenly coat. The mixture should be nice and saucy.

4. In a large bowl, combine the green cabbage, red cabbage, daikon, jicama, carrots, onions, and the remaining green onions. Add the mayo and rice vinegar and toss to coat.

5. Brush egg wash around half of the circumference of the edge of each round of crust. Evenly divide the pulled pork among the 8 rounds, piling it in the middle of each circle. Top each round with the slaw. Gently fold each handpie in half and seal using a pastry roller, the back of a fork, or your fingers. Brush the entire tops with egg wash, then sprinkle with the black sesame seeds. Cut 2 or 3 small slits in the top of each to vent. Chill for 30 minutes in the fridge or 15 minutes in the freezer before baking.

6. Preheat the oven to 350°F. Evenly place the handpies on the prepared baking sheet.

7. Bake for 35 to 40 minutes, until golden brown. Remove from the oven and serve. Caution, they will be super hot!

I was inspired to create a pie version of this classic sandwich because juicy smoked meat paired with melted cheese, hot mustard, and sauerkraut was an interesting new challenge. I could just picture it in my head and I had to make it happen. I was so delighted with the way it turned out (100% picture worthy) and even more so how it tasted. Yes, please!

MONTREAL SMOKED MEAT HANDPIES

MAKES 8 HANDPIES

½ recipe Double Butter Crust
(page 20)

Egg Wash (page 43)

1¾ lb (800 g) Montreal smoked
meat, thinly sliced

½ cup (125 mL) grainy Dijon
mustard

2 cups sauerkraut, well drained

2 cups (240 g) grated
Swiss cheese

Pickles, to serve

1. Prepare a single 9-inch Double Butter Crust, and cut into eight 7-inch rounds. Chill the dough until you're ready to assemble your handpies. Line a baking sheet with parchment paper.

2. Place the pie crust rounds on the prepared sheet, and brush half the circumference of each with egg wash. Divide the meat evenly among all the rounds, piling it onto half of each circle. Cover each with about 1 tsp of mustard and divide the sauerkraut and cheese evenly between the rounds. Carefully fold each handpie in half. Seal the edges with a pastry wheel, the back of a fork, or by pinching firmly with your fingers. Brush the tops completely with the egg wash. Cut 2 or 3 small slits in the top of each to vent. Chill the handpies for 30 minutes in the fridge or 15 minutes in the freezer before baking.

3. Preheat the oven to 350°F. Evenly place the handpies on the prepared sheet.

4. Bake the pies for 30 to 35 minutes, until the crust is golden brown. Serve with a pickle.

note Handpies freeze very well before they are baked (read more on page 229.). Keep a few extra in your freezer for super-easy lunches and dinners. You will be happy you did!

The mom in me named this chapter! There are a few things you don't realize you'll say all the time until you are a parent. One of those things is "eat your veggies!" and it's said on the daily in my house. I have tried all sorts of things to get my daughter to eat her veggies, and definitely resorted to bribery. In this chapter we take those veggies and turn them into delicious pie! You'll never have to beg anyone to eat veggies again when they are wrapped in delicious pastry and quite often a lot of cheese!

This pie is not just for kids, because, let's face it, who doesn't love super-cheesy mac and cheese? That cheese pull is everything! What makes it even better is to bake it in a Double Butter Crust. This pie is basically the ultimate comfort food—it's carbs, carbs, and even more carbs.

MAC & CHEESE PIE

MAKES ONE 9-INCH SINGLE-CRUST PIE

½ recipe Double Butter Crust (page 20)

3½ cups (454 g) elbow macaroni noodles

4 cups (400 g) grated sharp cheddar cheese

2 cups (255 g) grated Gruyère cheese

½ cup (114 g) butter

½ cup (75 g) flour

2¼ cups (560 mL) milk

2½ cups (625 mL) half and half

2 tsp salt

½ tsp white pepper

½ Tbsp prepared yellow mustard

¼ tsp paprika

note There's no one right way to make mac and cheese, and so many variations out there you can try—follow my super-creamy mac and cheese recipe, or use your own favorite in its place.

1. Prepare a single 9-inch Double Butter Crust and partially blind bake (page 24). Chill in the pie plate until ready to assemble your pie. Preheat the oven to 350°F. Line a baking sheet with parchment paper.

2. Bring a large pot of salted water to a boil and add the noodles. These will be baked later, so you only need to cook them al dente. *Tip: Set a timer for 2 minutes less than the recommended cooking time on the package. We find 5 to 7 minutes is usually perfect.* Drain the pasta and rinse with cold water to stop the cooking. Give the colander a good shake to drain all excess water.

3. Combine the grated cheeses in a large bowl.

4. In a large saucepan over medium-high heat, melt the butter. Once melted, sprinkle in the flour and whisk together to form a paste. Continue to stir for 30 to 60 seconds, then slowly pour in the milk, whisking the whole time to break apart any lumps that might form. Add the half and half and keep stirring to get a nice smooth consistency. Reduce the heat to medium and continue to cook, stirring constantly. The mixture should become thick and creamy.

5. Stir in the salt, pepper, mustard, and paprika, and about 2½ cups of the cheese. Once the cheese is melted, add another cup. Stir until this cheese has melted and then remove from the heat. Add the cooked noodles and stir to evenly coat. Cool to room temperature.

6. To assemble the pie, take the pie shell and fill it one-third full with your creamy mac and cheese, then top with 1 cup of grated cheese. Then fill the pie with the remaining mac and cheese and top with the remaining 1½ cups of cheese. Place the pie plate on the prepared baking sheet.

7. Bake for 20 to 25 minutes. If you love crispy cheese on top (who doesn't?) turn the oven to broil for the last 5 minutes, but watch it carefully to prevent burning! Remove from the oven, and let cool for 10 minutes before serving. This pie is creamy and will be messy to cut, but oh so yummy.

hen I first brought this creation home from the bakery to my number-one test subject (my husband), I was hesitant to share it with him. It is a vegetarian pie, and he's definitely a meat and potatoes kind of guy. But a few bites in he claimed that it was challenging his current favorite meat pie! I was shocked, but, hey, what's not to love about super-creamy-cheese-loaded potatoes with leeks in an all-butter pastry?

GRUYÈRE, LEEK & POTATO PIE

MAKES ONE 9-INCH DOUBLE-CRUST PIE

1 recipe Double Butter Crust (page 20)

3 large russet potatoes, peeled and sliced into ¼-inch-thick pieces

3 stalks leeks, washed and diced

3 Tbsp butter

2 Tbsp flour

¾ cup (175 mL) milk

1 cup (130 g) grated Gruyère cheese

1 tsp salt

¼ tsp white pepper

1 tsp lemon juice

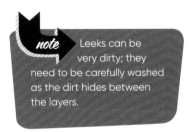

note Leeks can be very dirty; they need to be carefully washed as the dirt hides between the layers.

1. Prepare a double 9-inch Double Butter Crust. Chill the dough (bottom shell in the pie plate) until ready to assemble your pie. Line a baking sheet with parchment paper.

2. Bring a large pot of salted water to a boil. Add the potatoes and cook until just becoming tender, 8 to 10 minutes. Drain and let cool to room temperature.

3. Cook the leeks in a large pot with the butter over medium heat until soft and tender, about 7 minutes. Add the flour and mix to evenly coat the leeks. Cook for 30 to 60 seconds. Add the milk and stir well. Continue to cook until the mixture thickens. Add the Gruyère cheese, salt, pepper, and lemon juice. Stir until the cheese has melted, then remove from the heat and allow to cool.

4. Add the sliced potatoes to the bottom pie shell, filling the pie one-quarter full. Next, add a layer of the leek mixture to fill the pie half full. Repeat this process with the remaining potatoes and leeks, and smooth out to be nice and even.

5. Follow the steps for adding the top crust (page 24). Lightly score the dough (not cutting through) with diagonal lines using a paring knife (this is purely for aesthetics). Then cut four 1-inch slits to vent the pie. Chill the pie for 30 minutes in the fridge or 15 minutes in the freezer before baking. Preheat the oven to 350°F. Place the pie on the prepared baking sheet.

6. Bake for 60 to 70 minutes until the top is golden brown; some of the filling may start to bubble out of the vent holes. Remove from the oven and let cool for 10 to 15 minutes as it will be extremely hot.

his recipe creates a perfectly light pie, ideal for spring, an afternoon brunch, or to bring along to any potluck. The combination of thinly sliced potatoes, cheese, cream, and herbs is a definite crowd pleaser.

POTATO, CHEESE, SHALLOT & HERB PIE

MAKES ONE 9-INCH SINGLE-CRUST PIE

½ recipe Double Butter Crust (page 20), hanging several inches over the edge of the pie plate

5–6 small/medium white potatoes, thinly sliced into ¼-inch-thick slices

2 Tbsp butter

5 shallots, thinly sliced into ¼-inch-thick slices

2 cloves garlic, peeled and minced

1½ cups (375 mL) heavy cream

2 egg yolks

2 Tbsp chopped chives

1 Tbsp chopped thyme + 1 sprig thyme, for garnish

¼ tsp ground nutmeg

½ tsp salt

¼ tsp pepper

1 cup (130 g) grated Emmentaler cheese

Egg Wash (page 43)

1. Prepare a single 9-inch Double Butter Crust with 2 to 3 inches of dough hanging over the edge of the pie plate. Chill in the pie plate until ready to assemble your pie. Line a baking sheet with parchment paper.

2. Bring a large pot of salted water to a boil. Add the potatoes and cook until tender, 8 to 10 minutes. Drain and let cool.

3. In a large skillet over medium heat, melt the butter and sauté the shallots and garlic until softened and turning golden. Allow to cool.

4. In a large bowl, lightly beat together the cream, egg yolks, chives, thyme, nutmeg, salt, and pepper.

5. Fill the pie shell half full with the cooked potatoes. Top with the shallot mixture, then half the grated cheese, then another layer of potatoes. Cover with the cream mixture. Fold the edges up over the filling for a rustic look. Brush the whole surface of the pie crust with egg wash and top the exposed potatoes with the remaining cheese, a sprig of thyme, and some salt and pepper. Chill the pie for 30 minutes in the fridge or 15 minutes in the freezer before baking.

6. Preheat the oven to 350°F. Transfer the pie to the prepared baking sheet.

7. Bake for 60 to 70 minutes, until golden brown. Remove from the oven and let cool for 10 to 15 minutes before serving.

A twist on a traditional Greek spanakopita. Instead of the phyllo dough often associated with this classic dish, we use our Double Butter Crust, along with lots of spinach with caramelized onions and garlic, three kinds of cheese, and fresh herbs. This pie is perfect for not only your vegetarian friends, but everyone else as well.

SPINACH & FETA PIE

MAKES ONE 9-INCH DOUBLE-CRUST PIE

1 recipe Double Butter Crust (page 20)

⅓ cup (76 g) butter

1 onion, peeled and diced

2 cloves minced garlic

12 cups fresh spinach, chopped

1⅓ cups (305 g) ricotta

2 cups (200 g) grated mozzarella cheese

10½ oz (300 g) feta cheese

3 eggs

1 Tbsp chopped dill

1½ Tbsp chopped parsley

1 tsp salt

1 tsp pepper

1. Prepare a double 9-inch Double Butter Crust. Chill the dough (bottom shell in the pie plate) until ready to assemble your pie. Line a baking sheet with parchment paper.

2. In a medium frying pan over medium-high heat, sauté the butter, onions, and garlic until translucent. Let cool.

3. In a large bowl, combine the spinach with the ricotta, mozzarella, feta, eggs, dill (reserve a pinch for garnish), parsley (reserve a pinch for garnish), salt, and pepper. Add the cooled onion mixture and mix thoroughly.

4. Add the spinach filling to the bottom pie shell and smooth it out to make a nice even top. Follow the steps for adding the top crust (page 24) and sprinkle with the reserved chopped dill and parsley. Then cut four 1-inch slits to vent the pie. Chill the pie for 30 minutes in the fridge or 15 minutes in the freezer before baking.

5. Preheat the oven to 350°F. Transfer the pie to the prepared baking sheet.

6. Bake for 60 to 70 minutes, until the top is golden brown; some of the filling may start to bubble out of the vent holes. Remove from the oven and allow to cool for 10 to 15 minutes, as it will be extremely hot.

es, this pie has a lot of ingredients, but it is well worth the effort! The roasted yams and cinnamon give a little sweetness, while the other spices blend with the roasted peppers to provide some savory heat. To make this recipe vegan, just leave out the cream cheese and use a double Vegan Pie Crust (page 25).

MOROCCAN CHICKPEA PIE

MAKES ONE 9-INCH DOUBLE-CRUST PIE

1 recipe Double Butter Crust (page 20)

2 cups peeled and diced yams

1 red onion peeled and diced

1 medium red pepper, diced

1 medium yellow pepper, diced

1½ Tbsp ground coriander

1½ tsp salt

1½ tsp cumin

1½ tsp garam masala

1 tsp pepper

½ tsp cayenne pepper

Pinch cinnamon

3 Tbsp oil

One 19 oz (540 mL) can chickpeas, drained

2 medium tomatoes, diced

½ cup (114 g) cream cheese

¾ cup fresh or frozen peas

2 cups fresh spinach, coarsely chopped

1½ tsp lemon juice

1. Prepare a double 9-inch Double Butter Crust. Chill the dough (bottom shell in the pie plate) until ready to assemble your pie. Preheat the oven to 350°F. Line a baking sheet with parchment paper.

2. In a large bowl, combine the yams, red onions, red peppers, yellow peppers, coriander, salt, cumin, garam masala, pepper, cayenne pepper, cinnamon, and oil. Stir to coat evenly. Spread the mixture on the prepared sheet and roast until tender, about 20 to 25 minutes. Remove from the oven and allow to cool.

3. In a large bowl, combine the roasted vegetables, chickpeas, tomatoes, cream cheese, peas, spinach, and lemon juice. With clean hands or a spatula, mix until all the ingredients are fully incorporated.

4. Add the chickpea mixture to the bottom pie shell and smooth it out so the top is nice and even. Follow the steps for adding the top crust (page 24). Cut four 1-inch slits to vent the pie. Chill the pie for 30 minutes in the fridge or 15 minutes in the freezer before baking.

5. Preheat the oven to 350°F. Line a baking sheet with parchment paper and transfer the pie to the prepared sheet.

6. Bake for 60 to 70 minutes, until the top is golden brown; some of the filling may even start to bubble out of the vent holes. Remove from the oven and let cool for 10 to 15 minutes as it will be extremely hot.

acked with loads of vegetables flavored with traditional Indian spices, these handpies make a great lunch—and the mini version is perfect for appetizers.

VEGAN SAMOSA HANDPIES WITH MANGO CHUTNEY

MAKES 8 HANDPIES OR 24 MINI-TRIANGLE PIES

½ recipe Vegan Pie Crust (page 25)

Mango Chutney

½ cup (100 g) organic cane sugar

¼ cup (60 mL) distilled white vinegar

1 large mango, peeled and cubed, or 1½ cups frozen cubed mango

½ small onion, peeled and diced

2 Tbsp golden raisins

2 Tbsp finely chopped candied ginger

¼ tsp minced garlic

Pinch chili flakes

note If you are making the chutney in advance and want to store it, pour the hot chutney into a clean canning jar, leaving ½ inch at the top, and seal the jar. To properly can the chutney for shelf-stable storage, place the sealed jar in a large pot with a rack on the bottom. Fill with enough water to just cover the jar. Bring the water to a boil and continue to boil for 15 minutes. Remove the jar from the hot water bath and allow to cool at room temperature.

1. Prepare a single Vegan Pie Crust, and cut into eight 7-inch rounds (or fourteen 5-inch squares). Chill the dough until you're ready to assemble your handpies.

2. For the mango chutney, in a medium saucepan over medium heat, combine the sugar and the vinegar and stir until the sugar dissolves. Add all the remaining ingredients and stir to combine. Bring to a simmer, stirring frequently. Cook until the juices begin to thicken, 30 to 45 minutes. Place in an airtight jar and keep refrigerated for 2 to 3 days if planning to use soon (see Note).

3. For the filling, bring a large pot of salted water to a boil over high heat. Add the potatoes and carrots and cook for 4 minutes, then add the cauliflower and cook for another 6 minutes. Add the peas and cook for 2 more minutes. Drain the vegetables and set aside.

4. Heat the oil in a large skillet over medium heat. Add the onions, garlic, ginger, and cumin and cook for 5 minutes, stirring constantly. Add the coriander, garam masala, curry powder, fennel seeds, cayenne pepper, salt, and pepper. Mix well to incorporate.

5. Add the cooked potatoes, carrots, cauliflower, and peas to the skillet. Mix well. Use the back of a spoon to mash some of the vegetables, but keep the mixture nice and chunky. Remove from the heat. Stir in the lemon juice and the cilantro, and let cool.

Filling

2 cups diced white potatoes,
    (½-inch pieces) (2 medium)

1 medium carrot, peeled and diced

1½ cups cauliflower florets
    (½-inch florets)

½ cup frozen peas

1 Tbsp oil

1 medium onion, peeled and diced

2 cloves garlic, peeled and minced

1 Tbsp grated ginger

1 tsp ground cumin

1 tsp ground coriander

1 tsp garam masala

½ tsp curry powder

½ tsp fennel seeds, crushed

½ tsp cayenne pepper

1 tsp salt

½ tsp pepper

2 Tbsp lemon juice

¼ cup chopped cilantro

2 Tbsp water, for sealing

3 Tbsp olive oil, for brushing

6. To assemble the handpies, line a baking sheet with parchment paper and follow the steps (page 229) for filling and preparing the handpies, adding 1 tsp of mango chutney to each. Follow the same steps if making the mini triangle pies, with ½ tsp of mango chutney. Fold on the diagonal to get samosa-shaped triangles. Transfer to the prepared baking sheet. Brush the tops with olive oil and cut a few small slits in the tops for venting. Chill for 30 minutes in the fridge or 15 minutes in the freezer before baking.

7. Preheat the oven to 350°F. Bake for 35 to 40 minutes for the large handpies and 25 to 30 minutes for the smaller triangles until golden brown. Serve hot with extra mango chutney on the side.

e took one of our favorite chicken pies and went plant-based with it—and the transition was way easier than you'd think! The flavors were all so developed and amazing that substituting tofu for chicken was a no-brainer. The creaminess of the original came from coconut milk and cream, so it was also very simple to just switch to all coconut milk for this plant-based version.

VEGAN THAI TOFU PIE

MAKES ONE 9-INCH DOUBLE-CRUST PIE

1 recipe Vegan Pie Crust (page 25)

1½ packages firm tofu (525 g/18 oz total), cut into ½-inch cubes

1 tsp garlic powder

1 tsp salt

2 tsp curry powder

1 Tbsp lemongrass, white part only

1 tsp minced peeled ginger

1 makrut lime leaf

1 tsp lime juice

2 Tbsp water

1 Thai chili pepper

1 Tbsp oil

1 small red onion, peeled and diced

1 medium red pepper, sliced into ¼-by-1-inch strips

1 medium yellow pepper, sliced into ¼-by-1-inch strips

2 tsp salt

1 tsp hot sauce

1 Tbsp mild curry paste

⅓ cup (50 g) flour

2 cups (500 mL) coconut milk

2 Tbsp chopped Thai basil

1. Prepare a double 9-inch Vegan Pie Crust. Chill the dough (bottom shell in the pie plate) until you're ready to assemble your pie. Preheat the oven to 425°F. Line a baking sheet with parchment paper.

2. In a medium-sized bowl, add the tofu, garlic powder, salt, and curry powder and mix well. Spread on the prepared sheet and roast for 25 minutes. Leave the oven on but reduce the heat to 350°F.

3. In a small food processor or with a pestle and mortar, blend the lemongrass, ginger, lime leaf, lime juice, water, Thai chili, and oil until it forms a paste.

4. In a large skillet over low heat, cook the paste, stirring constantly, for 1 to 2 minutes until fragrant. Be careful not to inhale as it is strong! Lower the heat to medium and add the diced onions. Cook, stirring, until soft and translucent. Add the red peppers, yellow peppers, salt, hot sauce, and curry paste and cook for another 2 to 3 minutes. You don't really want to cook the peppers, just warm them up a bit.

5. Sprinkle the mixture with the flour, then stir to completely coat. Cook, stirring, for another minute, then add the coconut milk and keep stirring until the sauce has thickened. Remove from the heat and stir in the chopped Thai basil. Fold in the roasted tofu cubes, season with salt and pepper and set aside to cool.

6. Add the filling to the bottom pie shell. Follow the steps for adding the top crust (page 24) but brush the whole top with one of the dairy-free washes such as oil, nut milk, or water (see page 43). Cut four 1-inch slits to vent.

7. Line a baking sheet with parchment paper. Transfer the pie to the prepared baking sheet.

8. Bake for 60 to 70 minutes, until browned. Let cool for 10 to 15 minutes before serving.

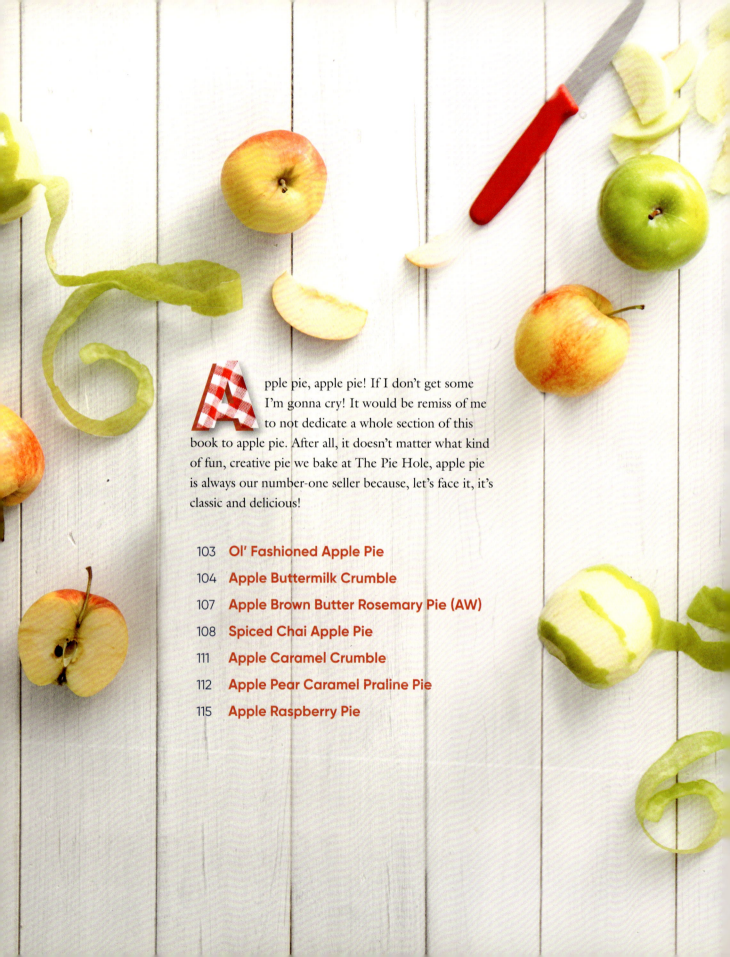

Apple pie, apple pie! If I don't get some I'm gonna cry! It would be remiss of me to not dedicate a whole section of this book to apple pie. After all, it doesn't matter what kind of fun, creative pie we bake at The Pie Hole, apple pie is always our number-one seller because, let's face it, it's classic and delicious!

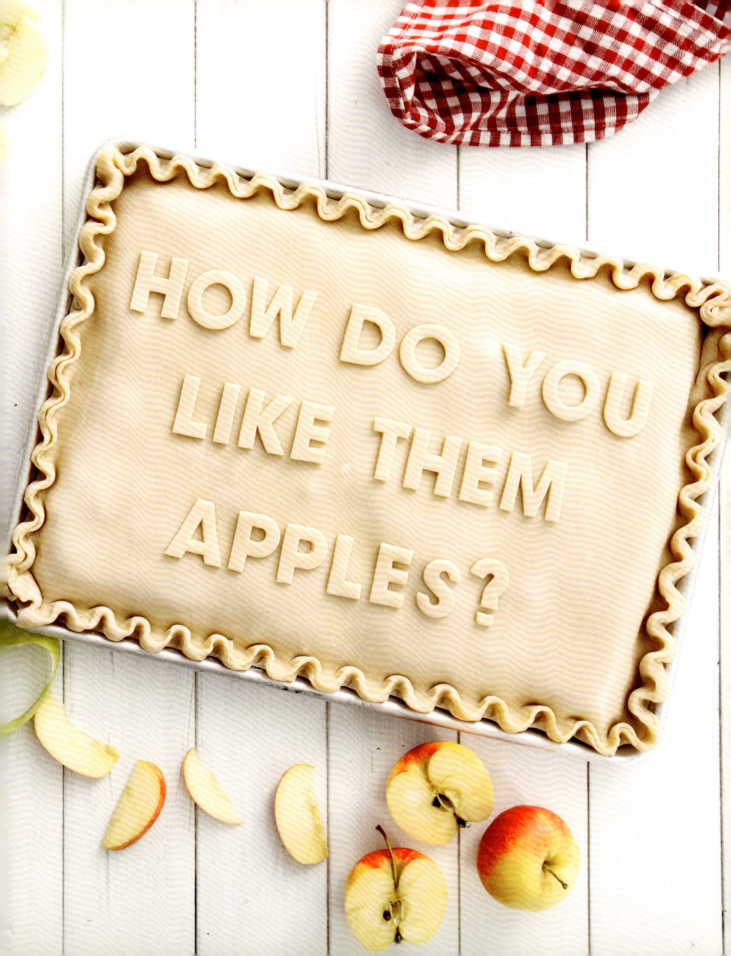

To Bake or Not to Bake: Types of Apples

At The Pie Hole we use a mixture of Granny Smith apples and Gala apples in our apple pies. That's not to say other apples don't make amazing pies; it's just our recipe. In fact, there are thousands of varieties of apples available! Here is a breakdown of some of the best apples to use in pie making. Note that these are more of the commercially available varieties. If you want to learn more and be inspired (and maybe overwhelmed), go to an apple festival and talk to the passionate farmers about heirloom apples—I've learned so much that way.

Granny Smith

Granny Smiths are readily available and one of the most popular apples for baking. The reason we use Granny Smith apples in our pies is because of their tart crispness. I love an apple pie that has distinct apple slices and not just apple goo.

Gala

We choose to use Gala apples in our pies. They have a natural mild sweetness, so we get to use less sugar. They also soften a little more than the Granny Smiths, giving a contrasting texture to the pie.

Gravenstein

These apples are a treat to bake with, but with a short season, they do not store well. If you see them at a market, grab a bag and get them into a pie stat! The flavor is both sweet and tart, and the firmness of the flesh holds well for baking into a pie.

Braeburn

Braeburns are sweet but have a subtle hint of spice. Try them if you like a heavily spiced apple pie with lots of cinnamon and nutmeg, as they will hold their own against the added spices. This very firm apple also holds its shape during baking. It doesn't release a lot of juice, so there is also less chance of a soggy bottom. For a bonus, these apples store well and can be found easily right through to spring.

Honeycrisp

As the name suggests, this is a nice sweet apple. Pairing it with a tart apple like the Granny Smith will give a wonderful balance in your apple pie. The flesh of the Honeycrisp is firm and holds up very well to baking.

Pink Lady

A very elegant name for an apple, Pink Ladies are very balanced between sweet and tart with subtle hints of honey and vanilla. They have a firm flesh that withstands baking temperatures, so they hold their shape and therefore the shape of the pie.

Jonagold/Jonathan

A classic apple for pie making because of the distinct mix of both sweet and tart flavors. Jonathan is the parent apple of Jonagold along with Golden Delicious. Both have a nice firm flesh that holds well to baking without turning to mush. These apples are in their prime at the beginning of fall.

Red Delicious

This section is called "To Bake or Not to Bake" and I would have to say that the Red Delicious, while they have a wonderful name, fall into the latter category. The flesh breaks down too much when baking, and it doesn't hold its shape. Red Delicious apples are best served fresh.

Melrose

A cross between a Jonathan and Red Delicious apple, the Melrose apple has a nice strong apple flavor and tartness, and it holds its shape well during baking, meaning it works very well in a pie. These apples usually hit their peak just after Christmas when the flavor has fully developed.

Crispin

These apples are also known as Mutsu apples. They are less tart than some of the others but with a nice firm flesh they bake beautifully in a pie. While they come into season during the fall, these apples store very well and can usually be found right into the spring months.

Fuji

A beautiful red apple with a nice firm flesh, crisp bite, and lots of juice, these apples are really nice for baking with. I recommend sprinkling a tablespoon of oats on the bottom of the crust to help absorb some of the juices from this apple and keep the bottom from going soggy.

Golden Delicious

These apples are naturally very sweet, and you can really let the fruit be the star of the pie and cut your sugar down a bit. They are not nearly as firm as some of the other apples listed so they don't hold their shape as well when baking. The flavor is great, and I would pair Golden Delicious with a nice firm, tart apple like Granny Smith to balance the flavor and texture.

Cortland

These apples are known for their beautiful snowy-white flesh. They are nice and firm and really hold their shape well when baking. So if you are looking for a lofty overstuffed pie, these apples work really well. They are not the most tart, but they do add a little tang to the pie.

Northern Spy

While these apples may not be commonly found at a grocery store, if you are lucky, you can find them at a farmers' market later in the season, especially more toward the middle to east of North America. They are the ugly ducklings of the apple world, not known for their beauty with their irregular shape and bumpy flesh, but because of their firmness they are wonderful for baking. Northern Spy apples are nice and sweet while still having a bit of tartness.

There is no pie more classic than apple pie. It sets the standard for what pie should be. It is also, in my opinion, the basis for telling a good pie maker from a bad one. The first year my shop was open, we were making pies as fast as we could. The demand was high, especially leading up to the holidays—in the days before Christmas the lineups were huge and the pies stacked high. Trying to be as efficient as possible, our staff were helping the first few people in line at the same time, and we accidentally committed the last apple pie in the shop to two different customers. What happened next was straight out of a newsclip about a Black Friday sale. The two women got into a physical altercation over the pie. I couldn't believe it, but I was also oddly flattered by the whole situation—knowing our apple pie is good enough to fight over.

OL' FASHIONED APPLE PIE

MAKES ONE 9-INCH DOUBLE-CRUST PIE

1 recipe Double Butter Crust (page 20)

4½ cups peeled and sliced (⅛ inch thick) Granny Smith apples

2½ cups peeled and sliced (⅛ inch thick) Gala apples

¼ cup (38 g) + 1 Tbsp flour

½ cup (100 g) golden sugar

Pinch nutmeg

Pinch salt

1½ tsp lemon juice

1 tsp vanilla

1 tsp cinnamon

2 Tbsp Cinnamon Sugar (page 254)

1. Prepare a double 9-inch Double Butter Crust. Chill the dough (bottom shell in the pie plate) until you're ready to assemble your pie. Line a baking sheet with parchment paper.

2. In a large bowl, combine the apples, flour, golden sugar, nutmeg, salt, lemon juice, vanilla, and cinnamon, and use a spatula to toss until the apples are evenly coated.

3. Add the apple mixture to the bottom pie shell and smooth it out to have a nice even top. Follow the steps for adding the top crust (page 24) and sprinkle with cinnamon sugar. *Tip: This pie also looks beautiful with a woven lattice top; see page 30.* Cut four 1-inch slits to vent the pie. Chill the pie for 30 minutes in the fridge or 15 minutes in the freezer before baking.

4. Preheat the oven to 350°F. Transfer the pie to the prepared baking sheet.

5. Bake for 50 to 60 minutes, until the top is golden brown and the fruit is bubbling out of the slits or the sides of the pie. *Tip: If you tilt your pie slightly and the juices flow out easily, it is not yet ready. Keep it in the oven for another 10 to 12 minutes until the juices bubble and are thick and gooey.* Let the pie cool completely before serving.

e don't do a traditional buttermilk pie, but we do a few twists on this old-fashioned pie, including this Apple Buttermilk Crumble. The sweet, smooth, creamy custard buttermilk filling pairs perfectly with the thinly sliced apples. We then top it with a buttery crumble.

APPLE BUTTERMILK CRUMBLE

MAKES ONE 9-INCH SINGLE-CRUST PIE

½ recipe Double Butter Crust
(page 20)

Apple Filling

4½ cups peeled and sliced
(⅛ inch thick) Granny Smith
apples

1 cup peeled and sliced
(⅛ inch thick) Gala apples

¼ cup (50 g) sugar

½ tsp cinnamon

Buttermilk Filling

¼ cup (50 g) sugar

2 Tbsp flour

¼ tsp salt

3 eggs

1½ cups (375 mL) buttermilk

½ tsp vanilla

1 batch White Sugar Cinnamon
Crumble (page 252)

1. Prepare a single 9-inch Double Butter Crust. Chill in the pie plate until you're ready to assemble your pie. Line a baking sheet with parchment paper.

2. For the apple filling, in a large bowl, combine the apples, sugar, and cinnamon and use a spatula to toss until the apples are evenly coated.

3. For the buttermilk filling, in a medium bowl, whisk together the sugar, flour, salt, and eggs. Slowly add the buttermilk and the vanilla, and whisk together until completely smooth.

4. Add the apple mixture to the prepared pie shell. Carefully pour the buttermilk mixture overtop. Top with 1 full batch of white sugar cinnamon crumble topping. Chill the pie for 30 minutes in the fridge or 15 minutes in the freezer before baking.

5. Preheat the oven to 350°F. Transfer the pie to the prepared baking sheet.

6. Bake for 50 to 60 minutes, until the topping has browned, the buttermilk custard has risen slightly, and the pie doesn't jiggle much with a gentle shake. Carefully remove the pie from the oven. Let cool completely before serving. As the pie is cooling, it is normal for the buttermilk custard to sink down, leaving an air pocket between the crunchy crust and the apple filling. Gently push the crumble back down as the pie cools if you see this happen.

note For an easy buttermilk substitute, combine 1 cup (250 mL) milk and 1 Tbsp lemon juice. Let stand for 5 minutes and voilà.

This is my absolute favorite spin on a traditional apple pie. Brown butter, in my opinion, elevates just about any dish. The nuttiness you get from the brown butter paired with chopped fresh rosemary perfectly accentuates the tart Granny Smith apples and the sweetness from the Gala apples.

APPLE BROWN BUTTER ROSEMARY PIE

MAKES ONE 9-INCH DOUBLE-CRUST PIE

1 recipe Double Butter Crust (page 20)

½ cup (114 g) butter

4 cups peeled and sliced (⅛ inch thick) Granny Smith apples

3 cups peeled and sliced (⅛ inch thick) Gala apples

1 Tbsp lemon juice

½ Tbsp lemon zest

¼ cup (38 g) flour

¼ cup (50 g) golden sugar

¼ cup (50 g) sugar

½ tsp nutmeg

½ tsp cinnamon

3 tsp chopped fresh rosemary (or 1½ tsp chopped dried rosemary)

Pinch salt

2 Tbsp Cinnamon Sugar (page 254)

1. Prepare a double 9-inch Double Butter Crust. Chill the dough (bottom shell in the pie plate) until you're ready to assemble your pie. Line a baking sheet with parchment paper.

2. To make the brown butter, in a small saucepan over medium heat, begin to melt the butter. Swirl the pot gently—there is no need to stir. Continue to cook until the butter starts to foam and turn brown and develops a nutty aroma. Remove from the heat and cool completely to room temperature.

3. Meanwhile, in a large bowl, combine the apples with the lemon juice and zest. Add the flour, sugars, nutmeg, cinnamon, rosemary (reserve a pinch for garnish), and salt, and use a spatula to toss until the apples are evenly coated.

4. Carefully pour the cooled brown butter over the apple mixture, leaving the dark fat in the pan, and stir to evenly coat.

5. Add the apple mixture to the pie shell and smooth it out to have a nice even top. Follow the steps for adding the top crust (page 24) and sprinkle with cinnamon sugar and a pinch of finely chopped rosemary. Cut four 1-inch slits to vent the pie. Chill the pie for 30 minutes in the fridge or 15 minutes in the freezer before baking.

6. Preheat the oven to 350°F. Transfer the pie to the prepared baking sheet.

7. Bake for about 50 to 60 minutes, until the top is golden brown, and the juices overflow and appear sticky. *Tip:* If you tilt your pie slightly and the juices flow out easily, it is not yet ready. Keep it in the oven for another 10 to 12 minutes until the juices bubble and are thick and gooey. Cool completely before serving.

There are certain things that remind me of fall. Wrapping myself in a big chunky knit scarf, kicking my way through brightly colored fallen leaves, sipping a hot cup of chai tea, and eating this pie. It feels like the perfect companion for a crisp fall day. I always recommend warming a slice a little and adding a scoop of your favorite ice cream.

SPICED CHAI APPLE PIE

MAKES ONE 9-INCH DOUBLE-CRUST PIE

1 recipe Double Butter Crust (page 20)

½ cup (75 g) flour

¼ cup (50 g) golden sugar

1 tsp cinnamon

1 tsp cardamom

½ tsp ground ginger

¼ tsp allspice

¼ tsp cloves

¼ tsp nutmeg

4½ cups peeled and sliced (⅛ inch thick) Granny Smith apples

2½ cups peeled and sliced (⅛ inch thick) Gala apples

¼ cup (85 g) honey

1½ tsp lemon juice

1⅛ tsp vanilla

2 Tbsp Cinnamon Sugar (page 254)

1. Prepare a double 9-inch Double Butter Crust. Chill the dough (bottom shell in the pie plate) until you're ready to assemble your pie. Line a baking sheet with parchment paper.

2. In a large bowl, combine the flour, golden sugar, cinnamon, cardamom, ginger, allspice, cloves, and nutmeg and mix well. Add the sliced apples, honey, lemon juice, and vanilla and use a spatula to toss until the apples are evenly coated.

3. Add the apple mixture to the bottom pie shell (it should be piled high and plentiful). Follow the steps for adding the top crust (page 24) and sprinkle with the cinnamon sugar. Cut four 1-inch slits to vent the pie. Chill the pie for 30 minutes in the fridge or 15 minutes in the freezer before baking.

4. Preheat the oven to 350°F. Transfer the pie to the prepared parchment-lined baking sheet.

5. Bake for 50 to 60 minutes, until the top is golden brown and the fruit is bubbling out of the slits or the sides of the pie. The juices flowing from the pie should be slightly thickened.

Tip: If you tilt your pie slightly and the juices flow out easily, it is not yet ready. Keep it in the oven for another 10 to 12 minutes until the juices bubble and are thick and gooey. Cool for at least 30 minutes before serving.

omemade caramel . . . drool! For those who like a little sweeter apple pie, this one hits home. Here you are smothering the apples in caramel before topping them with a golden sugar crumble—make sure you line your baking sheet for this one, as it will get messy!

APPLE CARAMEL CRUMBLE

MAKES ONE 9-INCH SINGLE-CRUST PIE

½ recipe Double Butter Crust (page 20)

3½ cups peeled and sliced (⅛ inch thick) Granny Smith apples

3 cups peeled and sliced (⅛ inch thick) Gala apples

¾ cup (150 g) golden sugar

3 Tbsp flour

1 Tbsp cinnamon

Pinch nutmeg

1½ tsp vanilla

Pinch salt

⅔ cup (150 mL) Caramel Sauce (page 258)

1 batch Golden Sugar Crumble (page 250)

1. Prepare a single 9-inch Double Butter Crust. Chill in the pie plate until you're ready to assemble your pie. Line a baking sheet with parchment paper.

2. To make the apple filling, place the apples in a large bowl. Add the golden sugar, flour, cinnamon, nutmeg, vanilla, and salt and mix thoroughly.

3. To assemble the pie, add half the caramel sauce to the bottom of the pie shell. Add the apple mixture and smooth it out to have a nice even top. Drizzle the remaining caramel sauce over the apples. Top with the crumble topping. Chill the pie for 30 minutes in the fridge or 15 minutes in the freezer before baking.

4. Preheat the oven to 350°F. Transfer the pie to the prepared baking sheet.

5. Bake for about 50 to 60 minutes, until the thick juices begin to bubble out of the sides. *Tip:* If you tilt your pie slightly and the juices flow out easily, it is not yet ready. Keep it in the oven for another 10 to 12 minutes until the juices bubble and are thick and gooey.

weet apples and the subtle flavor of pear elevate this pie . . . oh wait, plus there's the caramel and praline! This is next-level goodness! Perfect to serve warm with your favorite ice cream.

APPLE PEAR CARAMEL PRALINE PIE

MAKES ONE 9-INCH DOUBLE-CRUST PIE

1 recipe Double Butter Crust (page 20)

½ cup (125 mL) Caramel Sauce (page 258)

2½ cups peeled and sliced (⅛ inch thick) Granny Smith apples

2 cups peeled and sliced (⅛ inch thick) Gala apples

2½ cups peeled and sliced (⅛ inch thick) Bartlett pears

1 Tbsp lemon juice

3 Tbsp flour

¾ cup (150 g) golden sugar

1 tsp vanilla

1⅛ tsp cinnamon

Pinch nutmeg

Pinch salt

½ cup (75 g) Golden Sugar Praline Crumble (page 250)

1. Prepare a double 9-inch Double Butter Crust. Chill the dough (bottom shell in the pie plate) until you're ready to assemble your pie. Prepare the caramel sauce and set aside to cool. Line a baking sheet with parchment paper.

2. In a large bowl, combine the Granny Smith apples, Gala apples, and Bartlett pears. Add the lemon juice, flour, golden sugar, vanilla, cinnamon, nutmeg, and salt and use a spatula to toss until the apples and pears are evenly coated and the mixture appears a little wet.

3. Add the apple and pear mixture to the bottom pie shell and smooth it out to have a nice even top. Top with the crumble, reserving a tablespoon to sprinkle over the top crust before baking. Drizzle with the caramel sauce; if you like your pie a little less sweet, you can just use half. Follow the steps for adding the top crust (page 24) and sprinkle with golden sugar praline crumble. Cut four 1-inch slits to vent the pie. Chill the pie for 30 minutes in the fridge or 15 minutes in the freezer before baking.

4. Preheat the oven to 350°F. Transfer the pie to the prepared baking sheet.

5. Bake for 50 to 60 minutes, until the thick juices begin to bubble out of the slits and appear thick and sticky. *Tip:* If you tilt your pie slightly and the juices flow out easily, it is not yet ready. Keep it in the oven for another 10 to 12 minutes until the juices bubble and are thick and gooey. Cool for at least 30 minutes and enjoy!

I n the winter months, when you are dying for a little bit of summer, toss some frozen raspberries into your apple pie. In the summer, pick up some juicy fresh raspberries from the market, or better yet, go berry picking! Not only does it add a little pop of color, but it adds a robust pop of flavor. Summer or winter, it doesn't matter with this delicious pie.

APPLE RASPBERRY PIE

MAKES ONE 9-INCH DOUBLE-CRUST PIE

1 recipe Double Butter Crust (page 20)

3 cups peeled and sliced (⅛ inch thick) Granny Smith apples

2 cups peeled and sliced (⅛ inch thick) Gala apples

½ cup (100 g) + 2 Tbsp sugar

½ cup (75 g) flour

½ tsp cinnamon

Pinch nutmeg

Pinch salt

1 tsp vanilla

1 tsp lemon juice

2 cups raspberries, fresh or frozen

1. Prepare a double 9-inch Double Butter Crust. Chill the dough (bottom shell in the pie plate) until you're ready to assemble your pie. Line a baking sheet with parchment paper.

2. In a large bowl, combine the apples, ½ cup of the sugar, flour, cinnamon, nutmeg, salt, vanilla, and lemon juice and use a spatula to toss until the apples are evenly coated. Add the raspberries and gently fold them in, being careful the raspberries don't break apart.

3. Add the apple raspberry mixture to the bottom pie shell and smooth it out to have a nice even top. Follow the steps for adding the top crust (page 24) and sprinkle with the remaining sugar. Cut four 1-inch slits to vent the pie. Chill the pie for 30 minutes in the fridge or 15 minutes in the freezer before baking.

4. Preheat the oven to 350°F. Transfer the pie to the prepared baking sheet.

5. Bake for 50 to 60 minutes, until the top is golden brown and the fruit is bubbling out of the slits or sides of the pie. The juices flowing out should appear slightly thickened. *Tip:* If you tilt your pie slightly and the juices flow out easily, it is not yet ready. Keep it in the oven for another 10 to 12 minutes until the juices bubble and are thick and gooey. Let the pie cool completely before serving.

The majority of pies in this section are seasonal, as they require fresh fruit. Some of the seasons are short, so make sure to get your fill while you can!

n the early days of The Pie Hole, I loved to go and pick my own berries for pies. It is rare to find the time lately, but now I go mostly for the super-cute pictures of my daughter with blueberry-stained lips. Good thing they don't weigh us before and after picking at the local u-pick farms, because there's definitely some quality assurance sampling going on. And can you blame us with the berries so fresh and warm from the sun shining down on them? It really adds to the experience.

When choosing your fruit for pies, one must be picky . . . you want to choose ripe fruit, as it is the most flavorful. I believe that the fruit should be the star, and I love to let it shine as much as possible adding the least amount of sugar possible. Always try your fruit. Not all strawberries are equally sweet, for example, so sometimes you may need to adjust the sugar levels in the recipe a little. Moreover, as long as they aren't too tough, some fruit peels bake up beautifully in pie, imparting a lot of flavor and cooking down nicely. Peaches and plums are a perfect example—keep the skin on and just make sure to give them a very good wash. I also love the sour tartness that comes from leaving plum skin on. It is such a lovely contrast to the sweetness of the inside of the plum.

Blueberries are my absolute favorite berry. When I make a fresh blueberry pie, I always have triple the berries, as I am going to eat that many during the process! We only use fresh blueberries in our bakery for this pie. I find that frozen blueberries produce too much juice, and no one wants a soggy-bottomed pie!

BLUEBERRY PIE

MAKES ONE 9-INCH DOUBLE-CRUST PIE

1 recipe Double Butter Crust (page 20)

7½ cups fresh blueberries

1½ tsp lemon zest

1½ Tbsp lemon juice

1¾ cups (350 g) sugar

½ cup (75 g) tapioca starch

Pinch salt

1. Prepare a double 9-inch Double Butter Crust. Chill the dough (bottom shell in the pie plate) until you're ready to assemble your pie. Line a baking sheet with parchment paper.

2. In a large bowl, combine the blueberries, lemon zest, and lemon juice, and use a spatula to gently toss the mixture until the blueberries are evenly coated.

3. In a separate medium bowl, combine 1¼ cups of the sugar with the tapioca starch and salt. Add the dry ingredients to the wet ingredients and mix until evenly coated. The lemon juice will help the dry ingredients stick to the blueberries. Don't be afraid to crush a handful or two of blueberries, as they will burst anyway during baking.

4. Add the blueberry mixture to the pie shell and smooth it out to have a nice even top. Follow the steps for adding the top crust (page 24) and sprinkle with the remaining sugar. Cut several 1-inch slits to vent the pie. Chill the pie for 30 minutes in the fridge or 15 minutes in the freezer before baking.

5. Preheat the oven to 350°F. Transfer the pie to the prepared baking sheet.

6. Bake for 50 to 60 minutes, until the juices from the blueberries are bubbling and appear thickened. *Tip:* If you tilt your pie slightly and the juices flow out easily, it is not yet ready. Keep it in the oven for another 10 to 12 minutes until the juices bubble and are thick and gooey. Let cool to room temperature before serving.

ne of my favorite pies, but also one that intimidates people a little. Is it sweet? Is it savory? (Spoiler: it's sweet!) One day when I was late in my pregnancy with Cali I got a large phone-in pie order. They insisted on delivery no matter what the cost. The mystery of who these pies were for piqued my interest and I just couldn't say no. Driving with fresh-from-the-oven pies in your car is beyond torture, and as I was almost eight months pregnant, it was a miracle they arrived. It turns out I was delivering the pies to U2, rehearsing before their world tour! Later that evening I received a phone call from the president of Live Nation. They couldn't believe how amazing the pies were, especially this Blueberry Goat Cheese Basil Pie, and wanted to thank me by inviting me to the opening night of the show. Enjoy this pie and live life like a rock star.

BLUEBERRY GOAT CHEESE BASIL PIE

MAKES ONE 9-INCH SINGLE-CRUST PIE

½ recipe Double Butter Crust (page 20)

¾ cup (185 g) goat cheese

¾ cup (150 g) golden sugar

¾ cup (175 mL) heavy cream

2 eggs

⅓ cup (50 g) flour

Pinch salt

4½ cups blueberries, fresh or frozen (see Note)

¼ cup fresh thinly sliced basil

3 cups (450 g) White Sugar Crumble (page 251)

note If you are using frozen blueberries, keep them frozen until you are ready to use them. The more they thaw, the more they will dye your filling, and the contrast of the creamy filling and the blueberries is beautiful.

1. Prepare a single 9-inch Double Butter Crust. Chill the dough in the pie plate until you're ready to assemble your pie. Line a baking sheet with parchment paper.

2. In a stand mixer fitted with the paddle attachment, cream the goat cheese and golden sugar together. With the mixer running on low speed, slowly add the cream. Don't go too fast or it will get messy. Once the mixture is smooth and creamy, add the egg and continue to mix for 30 seconds. Add the flour and salt and mix for another 60 seconds until fully incorporated. Remove the bowl and use a spatula to gently fold in the blueberries and basil.

3. Add the blueberry goat cheese mixture to the pie shell and smooth it out to have a nice even top. Top with the white sugar crumble. Chill the pie for 30 minutes in the fridge or 15 minutes in the freezer before baking.

4. Preheat the oven to 350°F. Transfer the pie to the prepared baking sheet.

5. Bake for 50 to 60 minutes, until the crumble starts to brown, the edges raise slightly, and the middle of the crumble has a tiny jiggle and does not look wet. If the center of the crumble appears wet, with melted butter, keep baking for another 10 minutes. Let the pie cool completely, about 2 hours, before serving. If you make the pie in advance, store it in the fridge. Remove 30 minutes before serving and bring to room temperature. Do not reheat.

In late summer, when the peaches are at their juiciest from soaking in all that sunshine, and the blackberries are starting to dot the bushes, we love to make this Blackberry Peach Pie. This sweet and juicy pie is full of flavor and holds a little piece of my heart.

BLACKBERRY PEACH PIE

MAKES ONE 9-INCH DOUBLE-CRUST PIE

1 recipe Double Butter Crust (page 20)

1½ cups fresh blackberries

1 Tbsp cassis liqueur

5½ cups sliced fresh peaches

1 cup (100 g) golden sugar

3 Tbsp cornstarch

½ tsp ground ginger

½ tsp cinnamon

2 Tbsp Cinnamon Sugar (page 254)

1. Prepare a double 9-inch Double Butter Crust. Chill the dough (bottom shell in the pie plate) until you're ready to assemble your pie. Line a baking sheet with parchment paper.

2. In a medium bowl, combine the blackberries and the cassis, and soak for a minimum of 20 minutes.

3. In a large bowl, combine the peaches, golden sugar, cornstarch, ginger, and cinnamon and use a spatula to toss the mixture until the peaches are evenly coated and the cornstarch is fully dissolved.

4. Strain the blackberries and add them to the peach mixture.

5. Add the blackberry peach mixture to the pie shell and smooth it out to have a nice even top. Follow the steps for adding the top crust (page 24) and sprinkle with cinnamon sugar. Chill the pie for 30 minutes in the fridge or 15 minutes in the freezer before baking.

6. Preheat the oven to 350°F. Transfer the pie to the prepared baking sheet.

7. Bake for 50 to 60 minutes, until the top is golden brown and the juices flowing from the pie are bubbling, thick, and sticky.

Tip: If you tilt your pie slightly and the juices flow out easily, it is not yet ready. Keep it in the oven for another 10 to 12 minutes until the juices bubble and are thick and gooey.

love the topping of our signature Bourbon Pecan Pumpkin Pie (page 150), and just couldn't wait until pumpkin season to eat it again. This pie is its summer cousin, taking juicy locally grown peaches, topping them with toasted pecans, and finishing the pie with a little bourbon drizzle. I just love the textures.

BOURBON PECAN PEACH CRUMBLE

MAKES ONE 9-INCH SINGLE-CRUST PIE

½ recipe Double Butter Crust (page 20)

5 cups sliced peaches

1 cup (200 g) sugar

¾ cup (113 g) flour

1½ tsp cinnamon

¼ tsp salt

Pinch nutmeg

2 Tbsp lemon juice

1½ tsp vanilla

3 cups (450 g) Golden Sugar Pecan Crumble (page 251)

¼ cup (60 mL) Bourbon Drizzle (page 258)

1. Prepare a single 9-inch Double Butter Crust. Chill the dough in the pie plate until you're ready to assemble your pie. Line a baking sheet with parchment paper.

2. In a large bowl, combine the peaches, sugar, flour, cinnamon, salt, nutmeg, lemon juice, and vanilla and use a spatula to toss the mixture until the peaches are evenly coated.

3. Add the peach mixture to the pie shell and smooth it out to have a nice even top. Top with the golden sugar pecan crumble. Chill the pie for 30 minutes in the fridge or 15 minutes in the freezer before baking.

4. Preheat the oven to 350°F. Transfer the pie to the prepared baking sheet.

5. Bake for 50 to 60 minutes, until the peach juice is bubbling out and appears thick and sticky. Remove from the oven and let cool completely. Once cooled, top with the bourbon drizzle. You can serve this pie at room temperature or warmed up with a scoop of ice cream.

Fresh peaches from the orchard are the best way to go when making a peach pie. If you aren't lucky enough to live close to an orchard, fresh peaches from the grocery store will also work—just not frozen. The combination of juicy peaches with a touch of cinnamon is a little summer hug. Just peachy!

JUICY PEACH PIE

MAKES ONE 9-INCH DOUBLE-CRUST PIE

1 recipe Double Butter Crust (page 20)

7 cups peeled and sliced peaches

½ cup (75 g) flour

1 cup (200 g) sugar, plus more for sprinkling

1½ tsp cinnamon

½ tsp nutmeg

Pinch salt

2 Tbsp lemon juice

2 tsp vanilla

1. Prepare a double 9-inch Double Butter Crust. Chill the dough (bottom shell in the pie plate) until you're ready to assemble your pie. Line a baking sheet with parchment paper.

2. In a large bowl, combine the peaches, flour, sugar, cinnamon, nutmeg, salt, lemon juice, and vanilla and use a spatula to toss the mixture until the peaches are evenly coated.

3. Add the peach mixture to the pie shell and smooth it out to have a nice even top. Follow the steps for adding the top crust (page 24) and sprinkle with sugar. Cut four 1-inch slits to vent the pie. Chill the pie for 30 minutes in the fridge or 15 minutes in the freezer before baking.

4. Preheat the oven to 350°F. Transfer the pie to the prepared baking sheet.

5. Bake for 50 to 60 minutes, until the top is golden brown and the juices are bubbling out and appear sticky. *Tip:* If you tilt your pie slightly and the juices flow out easily, it is not yet ready. Keep it in the oven for another 10 to 12 minutes until the juices bubble and are thick and gooey.

PIE
MEMORIES

THE RASPBERRY CREAM CRUMBLE (PAGE 133)
was my go-to pie when I entered pie competitions. One summer, I was invited to participate in a local farmers' market pie competition on Vancouver's North Shore. I woke up early to make my pie. I was extra careful that my pastry would be a buttery, flaky perfection, and that each raspberry was carefully laid out so that as they baked, the bursts of crimson red contrasted through the smooth creamy-white custard. Once the pie was out of the oven and ready to impress, I picked up my sister to join me. I still remember driving down, the delicious smell of the pie wafting through the car, and joking how we should just pull over and eat it. It was torture.

We arrived at the market, a little later than expected, parked the car, grabbed the pie, and ran to get it onto the judge's table before the deadline. In true Parsons fashion we couldn't find where the drop-off point was. The clock was rapidly ticking and we had only minutes to spare. As our stress levels were climbing, we kept frantically searching. Was this the most secretive pie competition? It was seriously nowhere to be found. As the deadline came and went, I kept thinking, "Just a few more minutes." I then thought about what to say to the judges. "I am charmingly persuasive! I'll just apologize. Blame it on parking. Besides, how could they say no to this beautiful pie?"

I feared too much time had passed, and the judges must already be elbow-deep in pies. Feelings of disappointment and defeat crept in. Suddenly, it struck me, "Do I have the wrong date?" I sat on a bench, placed the pie beside me, and pulled out my phone to confirm the date while my sister continued to look. I reread the online invitation and realized the competition had been the previous weekend. I had missed it.

My sister walked up, smiling, and I didn't have the heart to tell her I had wasted her time. But I didn't have to. She knows me better than anyone. She held up two plastic forks she had grabbed from the food court inside the Quay and reached for my hand. We took that beautiful pie down to the pier. Sitting in the sun with a whole 9-inch pie, we dove in. We finished every last crumb of that pie as we talked, laughed, and enjoyed that moment together. My sister has always had my back and always will, and that moment, that memory, will always be with me.

Yes, this pie is amazing. But when you have such a strong, beautiful memory attached to it, that's when it becomes a true favorite.

hat to say about this pie? More like, what not to say?! It has won more awards than any other pie we make. It has become a customer favorite and even been featured on the very popular Food Network show *Diners, Drive-Ins and Dives*. The smell of it coming from the oven is out of this world, and the only bad thing is you have to wait a few hours for it to cool down and set before you can dive in.

RASPBERRY CREAM CRUMBLE

MAKES ONE 9-INCH SINGLE-CRUST PIE

½ recipe Double Butter Crust (page 20)

3 eggs

2¼ cups (560 mL) sour cream

1½ tsp vanilla

⅓ cup (50 g) flour

2 cups (400 g) sugar

¼ tsp salt

4½ cups raspberries, fresh or frozen

3 cups (450 g) White Sugar Crumble (page 251)

note Add 1 Tbsp of fresh zested lime to the sour cream custard for an amazingly delicious twist. This pie is best served at room temperature with fresh whipped cream.

1. Prepare a single 9-inch Double Butter Crust. Chill the dough in the pie plate until you're ready to assemble your pie. Line a baking sheet with parchment paper.

2. In a large bowl, whisk the eggs until they are light in color. Add the sour cream and vanilla and continue whisking until nice and smooth—no lumps!

3. In a medium bowl, combine the flour, sugar, and salt.

4. Add the dry ingredients to the wet ingredients and mix very well to fully incorporate.

5. Fill the pie shell with ½ cup of the sour cream mixture, or just enough to cover the bottom. Top with the raspberries and smooth it out to have a nice even top. Pour the remaining sour cream mixture over the berries, using a spatula to get all of it! Top with the white sugar crumble. Chill the pie for 30 minutes in the refrigerator or 15 minutes in the freezer before baking.

6. Preheat the oven to 350°F. Transfer the pie to the prepared baking sheet.

7. Bake for 50 to 60 minutes, until the edges have risen slightly and are set, the middle of the crumble is nicely browned and not too jiggly, and you can see juicy pops of sticky raspberry goodness. If the center of the crumble appears wet, with melted butter, keep baking for another 10 minutes. Let this pie cool completely before attempting to slice it, or it will be messy.

While making this pie might be the pits (get it?), it is worth the effort—I promise. Once you have your cherries pitted, the rest is easy. At The Pie Hole, our classic Cherry Pie is made with dark locally grown BC cherries. Sweet as Cherry Pie and might even make a grown man cry.

CHERRY PIE

MAKES ONE 9-INCH DOUBLE-CRUST PIE

1 recipe Double Butter Crust (page 20)

8 cups cherries, fresh or frozen

1½ cups (300 g) sugar

⅓ cup (40 g) tapioca starch

¼ tsp salt

¼ tsp nutmeg

2½ tsp lemon juice

1 Tbsp orange liqueur

note I love using a lattice top for cherry pies (see page 30), as it creates a peek-a-boo to that beautiful crimson color.

1. Prepare a double 9-inch Double Butter Crust. Chill the dough (bottom shell in the pie plate) until you're ready to assemble your pie. Line a baking sheet with parchment paper.

2. Destem the cherries and place them in a large colander to wash them. Use a cherry pitting tool to remove the pits. Be very thorough—no visits to the dentist!

3. In a large bowl, combine the cherries, 1 cup of the sugar, the tapioca starch, salt, nutmeg, lemon juice, and orange liqueur. Use a spatula to gently toss the mixture until the cherries are evenly coated. If you are using frozen cherries, set the mixture aside to thaw slightly so all the good stuff sticks to them, and stir after they have thawed slightly. Don't thaw too much or the mixture will get soupy before the tapioca starch has time to warm and thicken all that delicious cherry juice.

4. Add the cherry mixture to the pie shell and smooth it out to have a nice even top. Follow the steps for adding the top crust (page 24) and sprinkle with the remaining sugar. Cut several 1-inch slits to vent the pie. Chill the pie for 30 minutes in the fridge or 15 minutes in the freezer before baking.

5. Preheat the oven to 350°F. Transfer the pie to the prepared baking sheet.

6. Bake for 50 to 60 minutes, until the top is golden brown, the fruit is steadily boiling, and the juices flowing out appear thick and sticky. *Tip:* If you tilt your pie slightly and the juices flow out easily, it is not yet ready. Keep it in the oven for another 10 to 12 minutes until the juices bubble and are thick and gooey. Let the pie cool completely.

Let's not get "cherried" away, but it is my humble opinion that sour cherries make the best cherry pies! Sour cherries pack such a punch with a little sweetness and a whole lot of tartness. They are tricky little cherries to try to pit. A farm I get them from gave me a pro tip: float these little ruby-red gems in ice water while pitting them. It firms up the flesh a little and makes the job a smidgen easier. With the sourness of these cherries, I like to top this pie with a golden sugar crumble. The sweet and the sour is a heavenly combination.

SOUR CHERRY PIE

MAKES ONE 9-INCH SINGLE-CRUST PIE

½ recipe Double Butter Crust (page 20)

7 cups sour cherries

¾ cup (150 g) sugar

¼ cup (50 g) golden sugar

⅓ cup (40 g) tapioca starch

½ tsp cinnamon

Pinch salt

1 egg, beaten

1 Tbsp lemon juice

1 tsp Angostura bitters

3 cups (450 g) Golden Sugar Crumble (page 250)

1. Prepare a single 9-inch Double Butter Crust. Chill the dough in the pie plate until you're ready to assemble your pie. Line a baking sheet with parchment paper.

2. Float the sour cherries in ice water while pitting them. The cold helps firm them up and makes pitting them a little easier. Pit the sour cherries and place them in a large bowl.

3. Add the sugar, golden sugar, tapioca starch, cinnamon, salt, egg, lemon juice, and Angostura bitters and use a spatula to toss the mixture until the cherries are evenly coated.

4. Add the cherry mixture to the pie shell and smooth it out to have a nice even top. Top with the golden sugar crumble. Chill the pie for 30 minutes in the fridge or 15 minutes in the freezer before baking.

5. Preheat the oven to 350°F. Transfer the pie to the prepared baking sheet.

6. Bake for 50 to 60 minutes, until the top is golden and the juices are flowing out and appear slightly thickened and sticky.

Tip: If you tilt your pie slightly and the juices flow out easily, it is not yet ready. Keep it in the oven for another 10 to 12 minutes until the juices bubble and are thick and gooey. Let the pie cool completely before serving.

hen I think of strawberries, I am instantly brought back to my childhood. We had a little strawberry patch in the backyard that grew a handful of strawberries. Rather, only a handful survived thanks to a young bratty Jenell. With two tiny fists on my hips in protest, my number-one threat to my parents was that I was going to the yard to kick the heads off the strawberries. My mom still teases me to this day that we never got a chance to grow enough to make a pie.

At The Pie Hole, we get requests for Strawberry Rhubarb all year round. This classic pie epitomizes summer days and is best made using fresh ingredients only. The sweetness from the strawberries and the tanginess from the rhubarb is simply irresistible and brings back memories of a sassy little girl with squished berries on her toes.

STRAWBERRY RHUBARB PIE

MAKES ONE 9-INCH DOUBLE-CRUST PIE

1 recipe Double Butter Crust (page 20)

4½ cups fresh strawberries

5 cups chopped (½ inch thick) rhubarb

1½ Tbsp lemon juice

1½ tsp lemon zest

1 Tbsp vanilla

1½ cups (300 g) + 2 Tbsp sugar

⅔ cup (84 g) cornstarch

Pinch salt

1. Prepare a double 9-inch Double Butter Crust. Chill the dough (bottom shell in the pie plate) until you're ready to assemble your pie. Line a baking sheet with parchment paper.

2. Cut the strawberries in half, or quarter them if they are very large. In a large bowl, combine the strawberries, rhubarb, lemon juice, lemon zest, and vanilla and use a spatula to toss the mixture until the strawberries and rhubarb are evenly coated.

3. In a separate bowl, combine 1½ cups of the sugar with the cornstarch and salt. Add the dry ingredients to the wet ingredients and mix to coat evenly.

4. Add the strawberry rhubarb mixture to the pie shell and smooth it out to have a nice even top. Follow the steps for adding the top crust (page 24) and sprinkle with the remaining sugar. Cut four 1-inch slits to vent the pie. Chill the pie for 30 minutes in the fridge or 15 minutes in the freezer before baking.

5. Preheat the oven to 350°F. Transfer the pie to the prepared baking sheet.

6. Bake for about 50 to 60 minutes, until the top is golden brown and the filling dripping out is thickened. *Tip:* If you tilt your pie slightly and the juices flow out easily, it is not yet ready. Keep it in the oven for another 10 to 12 minutes until the juices bubble and are thick and gooey. Let cool completely.

notes This pie also looks beautiful with a woven lattice top (page 30). Pies like this with a high-contrast fruit color look so good with a lattice as it gives a little peek-a-boo to all the goodness inside. Plus, it allows the aroma of the fruit to escape and tantalize.

If you find your pie bottom is a bit soggy, next time try sprinkling in 2 Tbsp of "B"airy Dust (page 255) before adding the filling to the pie shell.

For those looking for something tart, this is the pie for you. I often explain this pie as awakening the taste buds. It has a subtle sweetness from locally grown juicy blackberries, a tartness from the rhubarb, and a little bite from the fresh chopped ginger. I cannot take credit for this brilliant flavor combination, which was suggested by a friend (thanks, Thane!).

BLACKBERRY RHUBARB GINGER PIE

MAKES ONE 9-INCH DOUBLE-CRUST PIE

1 recipe Double Butter Crust (page 20)

5 cups chopped (½ inch thick) rhubarb

4 cups fresh blackberries

1½ tsp finely chopped fresh ginger

2 Tbsp lemon juice

¾ cup (150 g) + 2 Tbsp sugar

⅔ cup (100 g) flour

note If you love ginger, feel free to double it up. This pie is amazing served warmed up and with a scoop of ice cream.

The photo here shows this pie in mini-size, and me having some fun with different decorations. Turn to page 30 for more on pie decorating tips.

1. Prepare a double 9-inch Double Butter Crust. Chill the dough (bottom shell in the pie plate) until you're ready to assemble your pie. Line a baking sheet with parchment paper.

2. In a large bowl, combine the rhubarb, blackberries, ginger, lemon juice, ¾ cup of the sugar, and the flour and use a spatula to toss the mixture until the blackberries and rhubarb are evenly coated.

3. Add the rhubarb blackberry mixture to the pie shell and smooth it out to have a nice even top. Follow the steps for adding the top crust (page 24) and sprinkle with the remaining sugar. Cut several 1-inch slits to vent the pie. Chill the pie for 30 minutes in the fridge or 15 minutes in the freezer before baking.

4. Preheat the oven to 350°F. Transfer the pie to the prepared baking sheet.

5. Bake for 50 to 60 minutes, until the pie is golden brown and the juices bubbling out appear thick and sticky. *Tip:* If you tilt your pie slightly and the juices flow out easily, it is not yet ready. Keep it in the oven for another 10 to 12 minutes until the juices bubble and are thick and gooey. Let cool for a minimum of 1 hour before slicing.

F reshly sliced pears are gently tossed with a beautiful blend of spices like cinnamon, ginger, and cardamom, and with a hint of maple syrup. This is a comfy, cozy pie that is perfect for fall or winter.

SPICED PEAR PIE

1. Prepare a double 9-inch Double Butter Crust. Chill the dough (bottom shell in the pie plate) until you're ready to assemble your pie. Line a baking sheet with parchment paper.

2. In a large bowl, combine the pears, sugar, flour, cardamom, cinnamon, ginger, salt, and nutmeg, and use a spatula to gently toss the mixture until the pear slices are evenly coated. Add the maple syrup and the orange zest and continue to mix.

3. Add the pear mixture to the pie shell and smooth it out to have a nice even top. Follow the steps for adding the top crust (page 24) and sprinkle with cinnamon sugar. Cut four 1-inch slits to vent the pie. Chill the pie for 30 minutes in the fridge or 15 minutes in the freezer before baking.

4. Preheat the oven to 350°F. Transfer the pie to the prepared baking sheet.

5. Bake for 50 to 60 minutes, until the top is golden brown and the fruit filling is bubbling out and appears thickened and sticky.

Tip: If you tilt your pie slightly and the juices flow out easily, it is not yet ready. Keep it in the oven for another 10 to 12 minutes until the juices bubble and are thick and gooey. Let cool for a minimum of 1 hour before serving.

Pears go so incredibly well with walnuts and cheese that I thought, why not turn that into a delectable dessert? This pie features a creamy goat cheese custard with thinly sliced fresh pears and is topped with a golden sugar and walnut crumble.

PEAR, WALNUT & GOAT CHEESE PIE

MAKES ONE 9-INCH SINGLE-CRUST PIE

½ recipe Double Butter Crust (page 20)

¾ cup (185 g) goat cheese

¾ cup (150 g) golden sugar

¾ cup (175 mL) heavy cream

2 eggs

⅓ cup (50 g) flour

Pinch salt

4 cups peeled and sliced (¼ inch thick) Bartlett pears

3 cups (450 g) Golden Sugar Crumble (page 250)

1 cup (110 g) walnuts, chopped

1. Prepare a single 9-inch Double Butter Crust. Chill the dough in the pie plate until you're ready to assemble your pie. Line a baking sheet with parchment paper.

2. Using a stand mixer fitted with the paddle attachment, cream the goat cheese and the golden sugar. With the mixer running on low speed, slowly add the cream. Don't go too fast, or it will get messy.

3. Once the mixture is smooth and creamy, increase the mixer speed to medium. Add the eggs and continue to mix for 30 seconds. Add the flour and salt and continue to mix for another 2 minutes until the mixture is super smooth and silky. Remove the bowl from the stand mixer and use a spatula to gently fold in the pears. Toss until the pears are evenly coated.

4. In a large bowl, mix the golden sugar crumble with the walnuts.

5. Add the pear and goat cheese mixture to the pie shell and smooth it out to have a nice even top. Top the pie with the walnut crumble. Chill the pie for 30 minutes in the refrigerator or 15 minutes in the freezer before baking.

6. Preheat the oven to 350°F. Transfer the pie to the prepared baking sheet.

7. Bake for 50 to 60 minutes, until the crumble is dry and starts to brown, the edges rise slightly, and the middle of the crumble does not jiggle too much with a gentle shake. Let cool completely, about 2 hours before serving. If you make the pie in advance, store it in the fridge. To serve, do not heat this pie up; just remove it from the fridge 30 minutes before serving to take the chill off.

There are a lot of pies that really benefit from the flavor and texture of adding nuts. Of course, the most classic of all is the Butter Pecan Pie (page 149). But don't feel limited to just adding nuts to a filling. You can also add nuts to a crumble—when the pie bakes, those nuts get roasted and even a little caramelized from the coating of butter and sugar. In some of the recipes in this chapter, like the Fat Elvis Pie (page 160), the nuts are incorporated into the whipped cream, and in others (like the Vegan Chocolate Hazelnut on page 167) they are crushed and pressed to form the base. You can use nuts to build a pie from the bottom up . . . and we are nuts about that!

oey gooey and full of nutty boozy goodness and sweet buttery filling. This is a very popular Southern-style pie that we load with pecans and set in our flaky Double Butter Crust. And if pecan pie isn't enough for you, you can take the classic and add chocolate, to make a pie for the serious sweet lover.

BUTTER PECAN PIE

MAKES ONE 9-INCH SINGLE-CRUST PIE

½ recipe Double Butter Crust (page 20)

¾ cup (170 g) butter, at room temperature

1¼ cups (250 g) golden sugar

4 eggs

2½ Tbsp flour

½ tsp salt

1¼ cups (310 mL) dark corn syrup

3 Tbsp bourbon

1 Tbsp vanilla

1½ cups (255 g) chocolate chips (optional)

3 cups (345 g) halved pecans

note I highly recommend serving this pie slightly warmed with either whipped cream or ice cream.

1. Prepare a single 9-inch Double Butter Crust. Chill the dough in the pie plate until you're ready to assemble your pie. Line a baking sheet with parchment paper.

2. In a stand mixer fitted with the paddle attachment, cream the butter and golden sugar. Once the mixture is smooth and creamy, add the eggs 1 at a time, mixing for 30 seconds between each egg. Add the flour, salt, corn syrup, bourbon, and vanilla, and continue mixing until thoroughly incorporated. Fold in the chocolate chips, if using.

3. Evenly spread the pecans across the bottom of the pie shell. Pour the bourbon mixture over the pecans. Don't worry, the pecans will slowly float up and become caramelized and crunchy at the top when baking. Chill the pie for 30 minutes in the fridge or 15 minutes in the freezer before baking.

4. Preheat the oven to 350°F. Place the pie on the prepared baking sheet and carefully transfer the pie to the oven. This filling is quite runny before baking, so steady hands are required.

5. Bake for 50 to 60 minutes, until the edges of the pie filling are set and the middle jiggles just slightly when you move the pie. Let cool before serving, which will help the pie set. You should serve the pie at room temperature or very slightly warmed.

have a confession to make: I have never liked pumpkin pie. That is, until I created this recipe. My solution was to add a toasty golden sugar and pecan crumble and drizzle the whole top with a delicious bourbon drizzle. Now we are talking! This became our signature pumpkin pie dish and has become a staple on Thanksgiving tables.

BOURBON PECAN PUMPKIN PIE

MAKES ONE 9-INCH SINGLE-CRUST PIE

½ recipe Double Butter Crust (page 20)

⅓ cup (76 g) butter, at room temperature

1 cup (200 g) golden sugar

2 cups (500 g) pumpkin puree

½ cup (125 mL) sour cream (room temperature)

2 tsp cinnamon

1 tsp nutmeg

½ tsp ground ginger

⅓ cup (42 g) cornstarch

¼ tsp salt

3 eggs

¾ cup (175 mL) milk

2 tsp vanilla

3 cups (450 g) Golden Sugar Pecan Crumble (page 251)

¼ cup (60 mL) Bourbon Drizzle (page 258)

note I find that this pie with all of its delicious spices actually tastes even better a day or two after it is made. The extra time gives the ingredients time to meld together. Just like a pot of chili, the flavor really develops as it rests.

1. Prepare a single 9-inch Double Butter Crust. Chill the dough in the pie plate until you're ready to assemble your pie. Line a baking sheet with parchment paper.

2. Using a stand mixer fitted with the paddle attachment, on a medium speed cream the butter until light and fluffy. Add the golden sugar and the pumpkin, and mix well. Make sure to scrape down the sides of the bowl at least once to make sure it is fully mixed.

3. Add the sour cream, cinnamon, nutmeg, ginger, cornstarch, and salt and continue to mix on a medium-low speed. Add the eggs and continue to mix well for at least 45 seconds. Add the milk and vanilla and mix for 1 to 2 more minutes until smooth and creamy.

4. Add the pumpkin filling to the pie shell. Chill the pie for 30 minutes in the fridge or 15 minutes in the freezer before baking.

5. Preheat the oven to 350°F. Transfer the pie to the prepared baking sheet.

6. Bake for 30 minutes, then remove from the oven and top with the golden sugar pecan crumble and bake for another 20 to 25 minutes, until the crumble is nicely browned and the pie does not jiggle too much with a gentle shake. Let cool completely.

7. Drizzle the bourbon drizzle over the top of the pie.

This pie must have the most asked-about name. One of the bakers, Colleen, mixed up two recipes, and the next thing I knew we had a hybrid version of chocolate silk pie in the oven. As it cooled after baking, the chocolate soufflé crashed down hard. What to do with this chocolate mess? I tasted it and knew right away that some maple candied pecans, caramel, and caramel whip would be the answer to this delicious "mistake." This recipe has had some revisions over the years (after all it had to replicate a "mistake") but the flavor is still to die for.

COLLEEN'S MISTAKE PIE

MAKES ONE 9-INCH SINGLE-
CRUST PIE

½ recipe Double Butter Crust
(page 20)

Chocolate Layer

¾ cup (175 mL) heavy cream

⅓ cup (80 mL) milk

2 eggs

1½ cups (255 g) semi-sweet
chocolate chips

¼ cup (50 g) sugar

Pinch salt

Salty Nuts

1⅓ cups (155 g) raw unsalted
pecans

1 Tbsp butter, melted

1 tsp sea salt flakes

Sweet Nuts

1 cup (115 g) raw unsalted pecans

1 Tbsp golden sugar

1 Tbsp maple syrup

¾ Tbsp butter, melted

Pinch salt

1. Prepare a single 9-inch Double Butter Crust and partially blind baked. Chill in the pie plate until ready to assemble your pie. Line a baking sheet with parchment paper. Preheat the oven to 350°F.

2. For the chocolate layer, in a large saucepan over medium heat, simmer the cream and milk. While the mixture is getting hot, in a large bowl, whisk the eggs until smooth. Once the milk is hot, add the chocolate chips and stir until completely melted. Whisk in the sugar and salt and mix well to dissolve.

3. Carefully, in a slow and steady stream, pour the hot chocolate mixture into the eggs, while constantly whisking, to temper the eggs. Tempering gently brings the eggs to a higher temperature without cooking them and making them lumpy. If you do get some lumps, you can use a fine-mesh sieve to remove them.

4. Transfer the pie shell to the prepared baking sheet. Fill the pie shell half full with the chocolate mixture and bake for 20 minutes or until the filling is set and does not jiggle with a gentle shake. Let cool completely.

5. For the salty nuts, add all the ingredients to a large bowl and mix thoroughly until the nuts are evenly coated with butter and salt. For the sweet nuts, add all the ingredients to a large bowl and mix thoroughly until the nuts are evenly coated with sugar, syrup, butter and salt.

6. Line a baking sheet with parchment paper. Spread each set of nuts evenly on one half of the prepared sheet. Bake for 15 minutes, tossing with a spatula every 5 minutes to help them roast evenly. Remove from the oven and allow to cool.

Caramel Pecan Layer

1 cup (200 g) golden sugar

1½ cups (375 mL) milk

1 egg yolk

1 Tbsp cornstarch

3 cups (450 g) Caramel
Whipped Cream (page 265)

> **note** I default to raw pecans to make my salty and sweet nuts but almost any nut, like unsalted peanuts, almonds or cashews, can work.

7. For the caramel pecan layer, in a medium saucepan over medium-high heat, mix the golden sugar and milk. While the mixture is getting hot, in a medium bowl, whisk the egg yolk and cornstarch until very smooth.

8. Carefully, in a slow and steady stream, pour ⅓ cup of the hot milk mixture into the egg yolk mixture while vigorously whisking to temper the egg. Tempering gently brings the egg to a higher temperature without cooking it and making it lumpy. If you do get some lumps, you can use a fine-mesh sieve to remove them. Add the tempered egg mixture back into the saucepan and bring to a boil while continuously whisking until the mixture thickens, about 5 to 7 minutes.

9. Remove from the heat and stir in the salty nuts. Allow the mixture to cool slightly and pour the mixture over the chocolate layer. Chill the pie in the fridge for a minimum of 4 hours or overnight.

10. Once the filling has set, spread 2 cups of the caramel whipped cream over the caramel pecan layer and smooth it out to make a nice even top. In a piping bag fitted with a round tip, add the remaining caramel whipped cream and pipe a border around the outer edge of the pie. Top the middle of the pie with the sweet nuts. Chill for a minimum of 2 hours before slicing.

Butter tarts, a Canadian classic, are the subject of much debate: to add or not to add raisins. If you are among the roughly 10% who insist they must have raisins in them, I am sorry, but I am just not a fan of raisins in desserts. When I started The Pie Hole, I made pies the way I liked them . . . and that has not changed to this day. I also like a firm butter tart, not the sugary-syrup-running-down-your-chin kind. With my Double Butter Crust, pecans, and a nice splash of Baileys Irish Cream, you will fall in love with them (even without the raisins). These are the number-one-selling item in our shops.

BAILEYS PECAN BUTTER TARTS

MAKES 18 TARTS

½ recipe Double Butter Crust (page 20)

1 cup (115 g) pecan pieces

⅔ cup (150 g) butter, at room temperature

¾ cup (150 g) golden sugar

1½ cups (375 mL) golden corn syrup

3 eggs

⅓ cup (80 mL) Baileys Irish Cream

1 Tbsp vanilla

1 tsp sea salt

1. Prepare the dough for a single 9-inch Double Butter Crust. On a floured surface using a rolling pin, roll out the dough until it is ¼ inch thick. Cut out 12 5½ -inch circles. This is the perfect size for a standard muffin pan.

2. Lightly spray a muffin pan. Gently push the dough circles into the pan; the edges will have to be pinched together at 3 or 4 points to fit. Divide the pecan pieces between the butter tart shells.

3. Using a stand mixer fitted with the paddle attachment, cream the butter and the golden sugar on medium-high speed for 30 seconds to 1 minute, until the mixture is nice and smooth.

4. With the mixer running on low speed, slowly add the corn syrup. Add the eggs, 1 at a time, and mix for 15 to 30 seconds between each egg. Add the Baileys, vanilla, and salt and mix until fully incorporated, 30 to 60 seconds. Do not overmix, as this can add too much air and prevent the pecans from rising to the surface while baking.

5. Pour the butter mixture into the tart shells. Chill the tarts for 30 minutes in the fridge or 15 minutes in the freezer before baking. Preheat the oven to 350°F.

6. Bake for 35 to 40 minutes until golden brown and bubbly. Cool for at least 30 minutes before serving. There is really nothing quite like a warm-from-the-oven fresh butter tart.

remember developing this recipe thinking, "How on earth do you make a plant-based version of a pie that actually has the word 'butter' right in the name?" As with a few of our other vegan pies, we use silken tofu. It blends so nicely and has a beautiful creamy texture. Topped with caramelized pecans, this pie is delicious.

VEGAN "BUTTER" PECAN PIE

MAKES ONE 9-INCH SINGLE-CRUST PIE

½ recipe Vegan Pie Crust (page 25)

½ cup (114 g) vegan butter

1½ cups (350 g) organic cane sugar

1¼ cups (310 mL) dark corn syrup

3 Tbsp cornstarch

3 Tbsp bourbon

1½ tsp vanilla

1 tsp sea salt

1½ cups (345 g) silken tofu

3 cups (345 g) halved pecans

1. Prepare a single 9-inch Vegan Pie Crust. Chill the dough in the pie plate until ready to assemble your pie. Line a baking sheet with parchment paper.

2. In a medium saucepan over medium heat, combine the vegan butter, sugar, corn syrup, and cornstarch. Cook until the mixture comes to a boil. Reduce the heat to low and cook for 1 more minute. Add the bourbon, vanilla, and salt and cook for 1 more minute. Remove from the heat and set aside.

3. In a food processor on pulse, blend the silken tofu until super smooth and creamy. With the processor running on low speed, carefully pour in the hot syrup mixture in a slow, steady stream. Let run for 30 to 60 more seconds to make sure the filling is thoroughly mixed.

4. Remove the bowl and blade from the food processor. Add the pecans. Stir until fully incorporated.

5. Pour the pecan pie filling into the pie shell, using a spatula to get all the filling out of the bowl. Chill the pie for 30 minutes in the fridge or 15 minutes in the freezer before baking.

6. Preheat the oven to 350°F. Transfer the pie to the prepared baking sheet.

7. Bake for 40 to 45 minutes or until the pie is set and does not jiggle with a gentle shake. Cool for a minimum of 1 hour before slicing.

This is one of the pies that got us all shook up! Taking some of the King's favorites, we came up with a delectable creation of chocolate ganache, banana pastry cream, and fresh peanut butter whipped cream, and finished it with more chocolate, caramel, and roasted peanuts. It's a *hunka, hunka* delicious pie!

FAT ELVIS PIE

MAKES ONE 9-INCH SINGLE-CRUST PIE

½ recipe Double Butter Crust (page 20)

1¼ cups (250 g) sugar

½ cup (75 g) flour

¼ tsp salt

3 cups (750 mL) milk

5 egg yolks

3 Tbsp butter

1½ tsp vanilla

1½ large bananas, mashed

1 batch Chocolate Ganache (page 261), warmed

3 cups (450 g) Peanut Butter Whipped Cream (page 265)

¼ cup (60 mL) Caramel Sauce (page 258)

2 Tbsp coarsely chopped roasted peanuts

1. Prepare a single 9-inch Double Butter Crust and partially blind bake (page 24). Chill until you're ready to assemble you pie. Line a baking sheet with parchment paper.

2. To make the banana pastry cream, in a medium saucepan over medium heat, whisk the sugar, flour, salt, and milk until smooth. Continuously whisk to keep the pastry cream from sticking to the bottom. Cook for 7 to 10 minutes until the cream thickens and nicely coats the whisk. The mixture will bubble as you cook.

3. While the mixture is getting hot, in a medium bowl, whisk the egg yolks until very smooth.

4. Carefully, in a slow and steady stream, pour about half of the hot and thickened sugar mixture into the egg mixture, whisking constantly, to temper the eggs. Tempering gently brings the eggs to a higher temperature without cooking them and making them lumpy. If you do get some lumps, you can use a fine-mesh sieve to remove them. Add the egg mixture back into the saucepan and slowly bring back up to a boil to thicken. Remove from the heat.

5. Add the butter, vanilla, and mashed bananas to the cream mixture and mix well to fully melt the butter.

6. Pour ¾ cup of the chocolate ganache into the bottom of the pie shell. Chill the pie shell for 15 to 20 minutes to allow the chocolate to set. Pour the banana cream mixture over the chocolate bottom.

7. Preheat the oven to 350°F. Transfer the pie to the prepared baking sheet.

8. Bake for 15 to 20 minutes. Remove from the oven and let cool completely.

9. When ready to serve, pipe or spread the peanut butter whipped cream over the top of the pie. Drizzle with the remaining chocolate ganache and the caramel sauce, and finish with the peanuts.

Can you believe it? I had never tried a Reese's Peanut Butter Cup. After years of being asked, I finally had to give in, for research purposes, and see what all the fuss is about. In an effort to come up with a pie reminiscent of this flavor combo and texture (which I have learned from avid fans is what makes these cups so desirable), I set forth and came up with this pie.

PEANUT BUTTER CUP PIE

MAKES ONE 9-INCH SINGLE-CRUST PIE

1 recipe Peanut Graham Cracker Crust (page 36)

1 cup (250 g) smooth peanut butter

1½ cups (340 g) cream cheese

2 cups (280 g) icing sugar

1 tsp salt

¾ cup (115 g) peanut meal or finely ground peanuts

1¼ cups (235 g) Chocolate Ganache (page 261), warmed

½ cup (75 g) Whipped Cream (page 265)

4 peanut butter cups, halved

1. Prepare a single 9-inch Peanut Graham Cracker Crust. Chill in the pie plate until you're ready to assemble your pie.

2. Using a stand mixer fitted with the paddle attachment, cream the peanut butter and cream cheese until light and fluffy. Scrape down the sides of the bowl as needed.

3. Continue mixing while adding the icing sugar a few tablespoons at a time, and add the salt. Mix until completely smooth. Add the peanut meal or finely ground peanuts and mix until just incorporated.

4. Add ½ cup of the warmed chocolate ganache to the pie shell and smooth it out to have a nice even top. Chill for 10 to 15 minutes to allow the chocolate to set.

5. Add the peanut butter filling on top of the chocolate bottom and use an offset spatula to spread evenly. Put the pie in the freezer for 30 minutes to allow the filling to set.

6. Pour the remaining chocolate ganache over the cooled and set filling, working quickly to spread it over the top. The pie should be cold enough to set the ganache quickly. If not, you can put it into the fridge until the surface is set enough that you can touch it and it doesn't stick to your finger (don't test this in the middle of the pie; no one wants to see a fingerprint!).

7. Once the chocolate ganache has set, decorate the top of the pie with 8 whipped cream rosettes, one for each slice. Press a peanut butter cup half into each rosette. Chill for a minimum of 1 hour before serving.

Trick or treat . . . hands down, this one is a treat! I love Halloween so much. I have a secret (maybe not so secret) dark side and love to play pranks, so I guess that is why I'm drawn to it. If you visit my shops, you will see them fully decked out with spooky, playful decorations, like our dearly departed skeleton friend who sits and enjoys a slice quietly in the corner. Chocolate, peanuts, and caramel—the ingredients for any good candy bar you'll find on Halloween—make for one delicious and decadent pie.

CANDY BAR PIE

MAKES ONE 9-INCH SINGLE-CRUST PIE

1 recipe Candy Bar Pie Crust (page 42)

1 cup (200 g) golden sugar

1¼ cups (310 mL) milk

1 Tbsp cornstarch

1 egg yolk

1½ cups (210 g) roasted salted peanuts

½ cup (130 g) Chocolate Ganache (page 261)

1 cup (150 g) Peanut Butter Whipped Cream (page 265)

¾ cup (113 g) Whipped Cream (page 265)

8 pieces mini Oh Henry! bar

1. Prepare a single 9-inch Candy Bar Pie Crust. Chill in the pie plate until you're ready to assemble your pie.

2. In a medium saucepan over medium-high heat, combine the golden sugar and milk.

3. While the mixture is getting hot, in a medium bowl, whisk the cornstarch and egg yolk until very smooth. Carefully, with a slow and steady stream, pour ⅓ cup of the hot milk mixture into the egg mixture, while vigorously whisking, to temper the egg. Tempering the egg gently brings it to a higher temperature without cooking it and making it lumpy. If you do get some lumps, you can use a fine-mesh sieve to remove them. Pour the tempered egg mixture back into the saucepan and bring to a boil, while whisking continuously, until the mixture thickens, 5 to 7 minutes.

4. Once the mixture is thickened, remove from the heat and stir in the salted peanuts. Allow the mixture to cool slightly.

5. Line the bottom of the pie shell with the warmed peanut mixture and smooth it out to have a nice even top. Chill for a minimum of 4 hours to allow the peanut caramel layer to set.

6. Spread ¼ cup of the chocolate ganache in a thin layer over the surface of the pie. Using an offset spatula, spread the peanut butter whipped cream over the pie's surface until smooth.

7. Decorate the top with 8 whipped cream rosettes and garnish each with a mini Oh Henry! bar. Drizzle with the remaining chocolate ganache.

This has become such a popular seller in our shops for both vegan and non-vegan customers. It is also one of my favorites, I think because I have convinced myself that it is super healthy and I can eat the whole pie! The rich creamy chocolate and the coconut whip with the texture of the pressed hazelnut crust is blissful. Try adding some of our Sour Cherry Compote (page 262) on top—it's like eating Black Forest cake.

VEGAN CHOCOLATE HAZELNUT PIE

MAKES ONE 9-INCH SINGLE-CRUST PIE

1 recipe Vegan Hazelnut Crumb Crust (page 39)

1½ cups (255 g) vegan dark chocolate chips

2 cups (480 g) silken tofu

¼ cup (60 mL) coconut oil

2 tsp vanilla

1½ Tbsp maple syrup

2 cups (300 g) Vegan Coconut Whip (page 267)

¼ cup (45 g) Toasted Coconut (page 254)

1. Prepare a single 9-inch Vegan Hazelnut Crumb Crust. Chill in the pie plate until you're ready to assemble your pie.

2. Melt the chocolate chips using a double boiler. Set up a pot with boiling water and position a heat-safe bowl to sit over the pot, not touching the water. Place the chocolate in the bowl and stir until the chocolate completely melts and is smooth. If you are using a microwave, use a microwave-safe bowl to melt the chocolate chips in the microwave, stirring every 30 seconds until smooth.

3. In a food processor, blend the silken tofu until smooth and creamy, about 1 minute. Add the coconut oil, vanilla, and maple syrup and continue to blend until combined. With the processor running on low speed, slowly add the melted chocolate and mix for 2 minutes or until fully incorporated.

4. Add the chocolate filling to the pie shell and smooth it out to have a nice even top. Chill for a minimum of 4 hours to overnight to allow it to set.

5. Decorate the top with some generous dollops of coconut whip. I like to keep the whip rustic and piled up in the middle of the pie, showing a little of the chocolate filling. Sprinkle with the toasted coconut.

CREAM OF THE CROP

My oh my, gotta love a cream pie. To me, cream pies are so classic, and I definitely could not have a shop without pies like Banana Cream (page 171), Coconut Cream (page 181), and Chocolate Cream (page 189). The pies in this chapter usually use a blind-baked pie shell and are filled with rich, sweet, velvety custard. Then that creamy and dreamy filling is typically topped with whipped cream. Cream pies are oh so decadent, and also perfect for throwing in someone's face . . . Just kidding! (Or am I?)

cannot make a cherry pop, but I sure can make a banana cream, and the name says it all with this pie. When I came up with this recipe, I wanted to make sure that the pastry cream packed a lot of banana punch. This was achieved with none other than fresh mashed bananas. That combined with sliced bananas, house-made whipped cream, a generous drizzle of caramel, and even more banana with the banana bread crumble makes for banana heaven.

TO DIE FOR BANANA CREAM PIE

MAKES ONE 9-INCH SINGLE-CRUST PIE OR FOUR 4-INCH SINGLE-CRUST PIES

½ recipe Double Butter Crust (page 20)

1¼ cups (250 g) sugar

½ cup (75 g) flour

¼ tsp salt

3 cups (750 mL) milk

5 egg yolks

1½ large bananas, mashed

3 Tbsp butter

1½ tsp vanilla

1½–2 bananas, cut into ¼-inch slices

1 batch Whipped Cream (page 265)

¼ cup (60 mL) Caramel Sauce (page 258) (optional)

3–4 Tbsp Banana Bread Crumble (page 253) (optional)

1. Preheat the oven to 350°F. Prepare a single 9-inch Double Butter Crust or eight 4-inch pie crusts, and partially blind bake (page 24). Chill the dough until you're ready to assemble your pie. Line a baking sheet with parchment paper.

2. In a small saucepan, whisk the sugar, flour, salt, and milk until smooth. Set over medium heat and continuously whisk to keep from sticking to the bottom. Cook for 7 to 10 minutes until the cream thickens and nicely coats the whisk. The mixture will bubble as you cook.

3. In a medium bowl, whisk the egg yolks until very smooth.

4. Carefully, in a slow and steady stream, pour about half of the hot and thickened sugar mixture into the egg mixture, whisking constantly, to temper the eggs. Tempering gently brings the eggs to a higher temperature without cooking them and making them lumpy. If you do get some lumps, use a fine-mesh sieve to remove them. Add the egg mixture back into the saucepan and slowly bring back up to a boil to thicken. Remove from the heat. Add the mashed bananas, butter, and vanilla and mix well to fully melt the butter.

5. Line the bottom of the pie shell with fresh banana slices. Pour the hot banana cream mixture over the bananas.

6. Bake for 30 to 35 minutes until the top firms a little and small brown spots appear from the sugars caramelizing. The 4-inch pies will bake for less time: 15 to 17 minutes. Chill in the refrigerator for a minimum of 4 hours before decorating.

7. Decorate the banana cream pie anyway you would like. We cover the top with piped fresh whipped cream rosettes, drizzle with caramel sauce, and finish with crumbled banana bread pieces.

This is the newest addition to our banana cream variations. We had the classic (page 171), we introduced the Fat Elvis Pie (page 160), but felt we needed a pie right in the middle, something that combined banana and chocolate sans peanut butter. With fresh banana-infused pastry cream, dark chocolate ganache, and mounds of whipped cream, who wouldn't be ready to dive in—or start swinging from the trees with a banana in hand?

CHUNKY MONKEY PIE

MAKES ONE 9-INCH SINGLE-CRUST PIE

½ recipe Double Butter Crust (page 20)

1¼ cups (250 g) sugar

½ cup (75 g) flour

¼ tsp salt

3 cups (750 mL) milk

5 egg yolks

1½ large bananas, mashed

3 Tbsp butter

1½ tsp vanilla

1¼ cups (325 g) Chocolate Ganache (page 261)

1½ large bananas, sliced ¼ inch thick

1 batch Whipped Cream (page 265)

10–15 dried banana chips (optional)

1. Prepare a single 9-inch Double Butter Crust and partially blind bake (page 24). Chill in the pie plate until you're ready to assemble your pie. Line a baking sheet with parchment paper.

2. In a small saucepan, whisk the sugar, flour, salt, and milk until smooth. Turn the heat to medium and cook for 5 minutes, whisking continuously to keep the pastry cream from sticking to the bottom, until the cream thickens and nicely coats the whisk. The mixture will bubble as you cook.

3. In a medium bowl, whisk the egg yolks.

4. Carefully, in a slow and steady stream, pour about half of the hot thickened sugar mixture into the egg yolks, while whisking, to temper the eggs. Tempering gently brings the eggs to a higher temperature without cooking them and making them lumpy. If you do get some lumps, you can use a fine-mesh sieve to remove them. Add the tempered mixture back into the saucepan and slowly bring back up to a boil to thicken.

5. Add the mashed bananas, butter, and vanilla to the cream mixture and mix well to fully melt the butter and incorporate these additions.

6. To assemble the pie, pour 1 cup of the chocolate ganache into the pie shell and put in the fridge to set for 15 to 20 minutes. Once the ganache has set, top with the sliced bananas, then pour the banana cream mixture over the chocolate layer.

7. Preheat the oven to 350°F. Transfer the pie to the prepared baking sheet.

8. Bake for 30 to 35 minutes until the top starts to firm up and brown spots appear from the sugar caramelizing. Let cool for a minimum of 4 hours or overnight in the refrigerator before decorating.

9. To decorate, using a piping bag fitted with the star tip, pipe whipped cream rosettes over the entire pie, drizzle with more chocolate ganache, and finish with the banana chips.

have had many phone calls over the years asking for Boston Cream Pie, which is actually a cake and we only make pies. Then my sister qualified for the Boston Marathon (cue big sister proud tears), and it only seemed fitting to finally make a pie version of this iconic dessert that claims to be a pie anyway. It came together much more easily than I expected, and ever since I served it, our customers keep asking for more. Side note: my sister crushed the race and had a personal best time!

CARLA'S BOSTON DREAM PIE

MAKES ONE 9-INCH SINGLE-CRUST PIE

½ recipe Double Butter Crust (page 20)

Cake Layer

1 cup (200 g) sugar

½ cup (125 mL) water

⅓ cup (76 g) vegetable shortening

1 egg

1 tsp vanilla

1 cup (150 g) flour

1¼ tsp baking powder

¼ tsp salt

1. Prepare a single 9-inch Double Butter Crust and partially blind bake (page 24). Chill in the pie plate until you're ready to assemble your pie. Preheat the oven to 350°F.

For the cake layer

1. In a small saucepan over medium heat, combine ½ cup of the sugar and the water and bring to a boil, stirring to dissolve the sugar. Remove from the heat. Measure ½ cup of the simple syrup and let cool. (If there is any extra, you can make a quick cocktail!)

2. Using a stand mixer fitted with the paddle attachment, cream the shortening and the remaining sugar on medium-high speed, scraping down the sides if needed, until the mixture is light and fluffy. Add the egg, vanilla, and the reserved ½ cup of simple syrup. Beat until combined.

3. In a separate bowl, combine the flour, baking powder, and salt.

4. With the mixer running on low speed, slowly add the dry ingredients, 1 to 2 Tbsp at a time, mixing between each addition.

5. Fill the pie shell one-third full with the cake mixture. Bake for 20 to 25 minutes, until the cake is set, and an inserted skewer comes out clean. Remove from the oven and let cool.

Boston Cream Layer

1½ cups (375 mL) milk

⅓ cup (66 g) sugar

¼ tsp salt

3 large egg yolks

3 Tbsp cornstarch

2 tsp vanilla

1 cup (260 g) Chocolate
     Ganache (page 261)

For the Boston cream layer

1. In a medium saucepan over medium heat, combine the milk, sugar, and salt. Stir and heat to a simmer. Do not allow the mixture to boil. While it is getting hot, in a medium-sized bowl, whisk the egg yolks and the cornstarch until smooth.

2. Carefully, in a slow and steady stream, pour about ½ cup of the hot milk mixture into the egg mixture, stirring constantly with a whisk, to temper the eggs. Tempering gently brings the eggs to a higher temperature without cooking them and making them lumpy. If you do get some lumps, you can use a fine-mesh sieve to remove them.

3. Using a spatula, transfer the tempered egg mixture back to the milk saucepan. Whisk continuously until the mixture thickens to a pudding-like texture and remove from the heat. Stir in the vanilla and mix well.

4. Pour the Boston cream layer over the baked cake layer and gently press a piece of plastic wrap to the surface. Chill for a minimum of 2 hours to set.

5. Warm the chocolate ganache just until it is pourable and cover the top of the pie. Put the pie back into the fridge to set. This pie should be kept in the fridge but served at room temperature. Remove 30 to 60 minutes before serving.

had a little tea party one afternoon at 3 and served this creamy, elegant pie topped with Chantilly cream and dried lavender. We use high-quality tea leaves and infuse the milk overnight to extract the lovely bergamot flavor.

EARL GREY CREAM PIE

MAKES ONE 9-INCH SINGLE-CRUST PIE

½ recipe Double Butter Crust (page 20)

3 cups (750 mL) milk

3 bags Earl Grey tea

¾ cup (150 g) sugar

½ cup (75 g) flour

5 egg yolks, whisked

3 Tbsp butter

¼ tsp salt

1½ tsp vanilla

1 batch Whipped Cream (page 265)

2 tsp dried lavender

1. Prepare a single 9-inch Double Butter Crust and partially blind bake (page 24). Chill in the pie plate until you're ready to assemble your pie. Line a baking sheet with parchment paper.

2. To get that beautiful Earl Grey flavor, in a medium saucepan warm the milk, but do not boil. Remove from heat and add the tea bags. Transfer to an airtight container and once the milk has cooled, put the lid on and steep for 4 to 12 hours in the fridge.

3. Preheat the oven to 350°F. Remove the tea bags and transfer the milk to a large saucepan. Add the sugar and flour and whisk until smooth. Over medium-high heat, bring the mixture to a boil, whisking constantly.

4. When hot and starting to get thick (about 5 minutes), carefully pour about ½ cup of the mixture into a large bowl containing the egg yolks, whisking constantly to temper the eggs. Tempering gently brings the eggs to a higher temperature without cooking them and making them lumpy. If you do get some lumps, use a fine-mesh sieve to remove them.

5. Return the tempered eggs and Earl Grey mixture to the pot and whisk continuously until the mixture has thickened (2 to 3 more minutes). Make sure to whisk all over to keep any spots from sticking and burning on the bottom of the pot.

6. Once the mixture has thickened, remove from the heat and stir in the butter, salt, and vanilla. Continue to stir until the butter is melted and the ingredients are fully incorporated.

7. Add the Earl Grey mixture to the pie shell and bake for 30 to 35 minutes until the filling has set. Cool the pie in the fridge for a minimum of 4 hours or overnight before decorating.

8. Using a piping bag and star tip, top the pie with whipped cream. Roll the dried lavender buds between your fingertips to intensify the lavender flavor and sprinkle them over the pie.

o shredded coconut here. All you need are coconut milk and cream to give you a dreamy, creamy silky coconut custard. If you want it to have even more coconut flavor, you can substitute Vegan Coconut Whip (page 267) and finish with the toasted coconut flakes.

COCONUT CREAM PIE

MAKES ONE 9-INCH SINGLE-CRUST PIE

½ recipe Double Butter Crust (page 20)

1½ cups (375 mL) coconut milk

1½ cups (375 mL) milk

¾ cup (150 g) sugar

¼ tsp salt

5 egg yolks

⅓ cup (42 g) cornstarch

1½ tsp vanilla

1½ Tbsp butter

1 batch Whipped Cream (page 265)

¼ cup (45 g) Toasted Coconut (page 254)

note This filling is gluten-free, so if you change the crust to the Gluten-Free Graham Crumb Crust (page 37) or the Vegan Hazelnut Crumb Crust (page 39), you will have a gluten-free pie!

1. Prepare a single 9-inch Double Butter Crust and fully blind bake (page 24). Chill in the pie plate until you're ready to assemble your pie.

2. In a large saucepan over medium heat, bring the coconut milk, milk, sugar, and salt to a boil.

3. While the mixture is getting hot, in a medium bowl, whisk the egg yolks and the cornstarch to form a thick paste. Mix until smooth.

4. Once the milk mixture is steaming, after 5 to 7 minutes of cooking, carefully, in a slow and steady stream, pour ¼ cup of the hot milk mixture into the egg paste, whisking constantly to temper the eggs. Tempering gently brings the eggs to a higher temperature without cooking them and making them lumpy. If you do get some lumps, you can use a fine-mesh sieve to remove them.

5. Using a spatula, return the tempered hot egg mixture to the pot. Bring to a boil over medium-high heat while stirring constantly. The mixture should have a thick, pudding-like consistency and hold a ribbon for at least 5 seconds.

6. Remove from the heat and add the vanilla and butter. Stir until the butter is melted and the ingredients are fully mixed.

7. Add the coconut mixture to the bottom of the pie shell and smooth it out to make a nice even top. Cover the surface with a piece of plastic wrap and set in the fridge for a minimum of 4 hours or overnight to allow the coconut mixture to set.

8. Decorate the pie with whipped cream rosettes and sprinkle with toasted coconut.

This pie is one of the new kids on the block for The Pie Hole. When I was picking up some takeout from a local Mexican restaurant, the guy working the front counter encouraged me to try one of their house-made horchatas. He was very passionate about it and it was a super-hot day, so I agreed. I hopped in my car and brought that straw to my lips, and it was love at first sip. Immediately, I pictured this drink turned into a pie. Not a day goes by that I am not thinking about some kind of pie creation, and you never know where that inspiration will come from.

HORCHATA CREAM PIE

MAKES ONE 9-INCH SINGLE-CRUST PIE

½ recipe Double Butter Crust (page 20)

Horchata Milk

⅓ cup (65 g) long-grain white rice, uncooked

2 cups (500 mL) water

1 cinnamon stick

⅔ cup (160 mL) milk

½ cup (125 mL) coconut milk

1½ Tbsp vanilla

1½ Tbsp cinnamon

½ cup (100 g) sugar

1. Prepare a single 9-inch Double Butter Crust and partially blind bake (page 24). Chill until you're ready to assemble your pie. Line a baking sheet with parchment paper.

2. For the horchata milk, blend the rice, ½ cup of the water, and the cinnamon stick on high speed in a small food processor or blender, for 2 to 3 minutes, until the rice and cinnamon stick are broken up a little. Add the remaining water and blend again for 2 minutes.

3. Transfer the mixture to an airtight container and leave at room temperature for a minimum of 8 hours.

4. Using a fine-mesh strainer, strain the mixture into a pitcher. Discard the solids. Stir in the milk, coconut milk, vanilla, ground cinnamon, and sugar. Chill in the fridge until ready to use, up to 3 days.

5. Preheat the oven to 350°F.

Filling

1¼ cups (250 g) sugar

½ cup (75 g) flour

¼ tsp salt

5 egg yolks

3 Tbsp butter

1½ tsp vanilla

1 batch Whipped Cream
    (page 265)

1 Tbsp Cinnamon Sugar
    (page 254)

6. For the filling, in a small saucepan, whisk the sugar, flour, salt, and 3 cups of the horchata milk until smooth. Set over medium heat and continuously whisk to keep the mixture from sticking to the bottom as it thickens. Cook for 7 to 10 minutes until the filling nicely coats the whisk. The mixture will bubble as you cook.

7. While the mixture is getting hot, in a medium bowl, whisk the egg yolks until very smooth.

8. Carefully, in a slow and steady stream, pour about half of the hot horchata mixture into the egg yolks, whisking constantly, to temper the eggs. Tempering gently brings the eggs to a higher temperature without cooking them and making them lumpy. If you do get some lumps, you can use a fine-mesh sieve to remove them.

9. Return the mixture to the saucepan and slowly bring it back up to a boil, stirring constantly to thicken it. This should happen in 2 to 3 minutes. Remove from the heat. Add the butter and vanilla and mix well to fully melt the butter. Add the horchata mixture to the pie shell and smooth it out to make a nice even top.

10. Bake for 15 to 20 minutes until the filling firms a little and the top browns from the sugar caramelizing. Don't worry if it doesn't look pretty at this point, as the whipped cream covers it. Let cool completely. Once cooled, cover with whipped cream rosettes and a generous sprinkling of cinnamon sugar.

A childhood favorite for most people. My mom never baked cookies when I was growing up; she was a great cook but not a baker. So, if there were cookies around the house, they were store-bought, hard, and unappealing. That probably explains why I wasn't really into cookies or dunking them into a cold glass of milk. But my husband loves cookies, and now that I've started making them for him, I have a real weakness for cookies too. I like to decorate the top of the pie with mini chocolate chip cookies. You don't have to do this, but I will include my chocolate chip cookie recipe just in case. I don't know if anyone has ever regretted making delicious cookies.

MILK 'N' COOKIES PIE

MAKES ONE 9-INCH SINGLE-CRUST PIE

½ recipe Double Butter Crust (page 20)

Cookie Layer

2 eggs

1½ cups (225 g) flour

½ cup (100 g) sugar

½ cup (100 g) golden sugar

2 tsp vanilla

½ tsp sea salt

¾ cup (170 g) butter, at room temperature

1 cup (170 g) semi-sweet chocolate chips

Milk Cream Layer

½ cup (100 g) sugar

2 Tbsp flour

Pinch salt

1⅓ cups (330 mL) milk

2 egg yolks

1 Tbsp butter

1 tsp vanilla

1. Prepare a single 9-inch Double Butter Crust and partially blind bake (page 24). Chill until ready to assemble your pie. Preheat the oven to 350°F. Line a baking sheet with parchment paper.

2. For the cookie layer, using a stand mixer fitted with the paddle attachment, beat the eggs on medium speed until they are foamy. Reduce the speed to low and add the flour, sugar, golden sugar, vanilla, and salt and mix to incorporate, about 2 minutes.

3. Add the butter, increase the speed to medium high, and continue mixing, scraping down the sides of the bowl when necessary, for 1 to 2 minutes. Add the chocolate chips and mix for another minute until just incorporated.

4. To assemble the pie, fill the pie shell about one-third full with the cookie dough. Starting from the outside and working your way in, carefully press the cookie dough down with your hands to line the bottom with a large cookie. Transfer the pie to the prepared sheet.

5. Bake for 15 to 25 minutes.

6. For the milk cream layer, in a small saucepan, whisk the sugar, flour, salt, and milk until smooth. Turn the heat to medium and continuously whisk to keep the pastry cream from sticking to the bottom. Cook for 5 minutes until the cream thickens and nicely coats the whisk. The mixture will bubble as you cook.

7. In a medium bowl, whisk the egg yolks until very smooth.

8. Carefully, in a slow and steady stream, pour about half of the hot thickened sugar mixture into the egg yolks, whisking constantly,

Chocolate Chip Cookies (Optional)

1 cup (227 g) butter, softened

¾ cup (150 g) sugar

¾ cup (150 g) golden sugar

2 eggs

2 tsp vanilla

2¼ cups (338 g) flour

1 tsp baking soda

1 tsp sea salt

2 cups (340 g) semi-sweet chocolate chips

2 cups (300 g) Whipped Cream (page 265)

½ cup (130 g) Chocolate Ganache (page 261), warmed

to temper the eggs. Tempering gently brings the eggs to a higher temperature without cooking them and making them lumpy. If you do get some lumps, you can use a fine-mesh sieve to remove them.

9. Return the egg mixture back to the saucepan and slowly bring back up to a boil to thicken. Remove from the heat. Add the butter and vanilla and mix well to fully melt the butter and incorporate the vanilla.

10. When the cookie is done baking, pour the milk cream layer over the hot baked cookie layer. Bake for another 15 minutes. Let cool for 30 minutes at room temperature and then chill for a minimum of 1 hour.

11. For the chocolate chip cookies, using a stand mixer fitted with the paddle attachment, cream the butter, sugar, and golden sugar on high speed until light and fluffy. With the mixer running on medium speed, add the eggs 1 at a time, beating for 30 to 60 seconds between each one. Add the vanilla and continue to mix well.

12. In a medium bowl, combine the flour, baking soda, and salt.

13. With the mixer running on low speed, gradually add the dry ingredients, 2 Tbsp at a time, blending in the ingredients before adding more. Continue mixing until the dry ingredients are fully incorporated. Add the chocolate chips and mix just enough to evenly disperse them throughout the cookie dough, about 30 seconds. Chill the cookie dough for 30 minutes.

14. Preheat the oven to 350°F. Line 2 baking sheets with parchment paper.

15. Using a teaspoon, form 8 mini cookie balls (about ½ inch in diameter) and spread evenly on 1 baking sheet. These will be used to decorate the pie. Set the remaining dough aside.

16. Bake for 5 to 7 minutes. Remove from the oven and let cool, then roughly chop.

17. On the other baking sheet, using a 2-ounce scoop or your hands, spoon the rest of the cookie dough to make regular-sized (2- to 2½-inch) cookies and spread evenly, 2 to 3 inches apart, on the baking sheet. Bake for 10 to 12 minutes. Remove from the oven and let cool, then roughly chop.

18. To decorate the pie, use a piping bag fitted with a star tip to pipe a ring of whipped cream rosettes around the top of the pie. Fill the center of the pie with the roughly chopped cookies. Drizzle with the chocolate ganache. Finish with the mini chocolate chip cookies evenly spaced in the whipped cream.

For Valentine's Day, we want your sweetie to feel extra love, so a single chocolate cream pie just won't cut it. Doubling it is not quite good enough either. We go all in with a triple chocolate pie, and at the Pie Hole, we dust it in gold! (Note: This pie is not just limited to V Day!)

TRIPLE CHOCOLATE CREAM PIE

MAKES ONE 9-INCH SINGLE-CRUST PIE

½ recipe Double Butter Crust (page 20)

¾ cup (175 mL) heavy cream

⅓ cup (80 mL) milk

1⅔ cups (285g) semi-sweet chocolate chips

¼ cup (50 g) sugar

Pinch salt

2 eggs

3 cups (450 g) Chocolate Whipped Cream (page 266)

3 cups (780 g) Whipped White Chocolate Ganache (page 267)

4–5 pumps edible gold dust spray (optional)

note Edible gold dust is completely optional, as it can be hard to source. But if you can find it, I suggest buying it! PS: I love shiny things! Alternatively, you can finish the pie with a drizzle of Chocolate Ganache (page 261) or sprinkle with some chocolate shavings or curls.

1. Prepare a single 9-inch Double Butter Crust, and fully blind bake (page 24). Chill until you're ready to assemble your pie.

2. In a large saucepan over medium heat, simmer the cream and milk. Once the milk is steaming, add the chocolate chips and stir until completely melted. Whisk in the sugar and salt and mix well to dissolve.

3. While the milk mixture is getting hot, in a medium bowl, whisk the eggs until smooth.

4. Carefully, in a slow and steady stream, pour one-third of the hot chocolate mixture into the eggs, whisking constantly, to temper the eggs. Tempering gently brings the eggs to a higher temperature without cooking them and making them lumpy. If you do get some lumps, you can use a fine-mesh sieve to remove them. Return the mixture back to the saucepan, and slowly bring to a boil to thicken it.

5. Pour the chocolate mixture into the bottom of the pie shell until half full. Bake for 20 minutes, until the filling is set and does not jiggle with a gentle shake. Allow to cool completely before adding the second layer.

6. Add the chocolate whipped cream and smooth it out to have a nice even top. Using a piping bag fitted with a star tip or just a spoon, cover with the whipped white chocolate ganache. Finish with a spray of edible gold dust.

This pie doesn't come with Grandpa's pocket lint. Our creamy and delicious butterscotch pie gets its rich flavor from blending melted butter, golden sugar, cream, and vanilla. We make it in the form of a pastry cream for this pie and top it with Italian meringue or fresh whipped cream.

BUTTERSCOTCH PIE

MAKES ONE 9-INCH SINGLE-CRUST PIE

½ recipe Double Butter Crust (page 20)

5 egg yolks

2¾ cups (675 mL) milk

1⅓ cups (266 g) golden sugar

¾ cup (150 g) sugar

⅓ cup (42 g) cornstarch

¼ tsp salt

2½ Tbsp butter

2 tsp vanilla

1 batch Italian Meringue (page 268)

1. Prepare a single 9-inch Double Butter Crust and fully blind bake (page 24). Chill until you're ready to assemble your pie.

2. In a small bowl, whisk the egg yolks and the milk.

3. In a large pot, combine the golden sugar, sugar, cornstarch, and salt. Set over medium-high heat and slowly add the milk mixture, whisking constantly. Bring the mixture to a boil and stir for an additional 30 seconds. You should have a thick pudding-like consistency.

4. Remove from the heat and add the butter and vanilla. Stir until the butter is completely melted and the mixture is smooth and creamy.

5. To assemble the pie, add the filling to the pie shell and smooth it out to make a nice even top. Cover with plastic wrap and gently press the wrap to the top of the filling. Chill for a minimum of 4 hours or overnight.

6. When the pie is chilled, top with the Italian meringue, nice and high, making sure to cover the entire surface. Push the meringue right to the edge of the pie crust, to protect the delicate filling when you torch the meringue.

7. Use a kitchen torch to carefully brown the meringue, or place the pie on a parchment-lined baking sheet on the bottom rack of your oven and broil for 3 to 4 minutes. Keep a very close eye on the pie, as it doesn't take long to burn the meringue. You can also top this pie with fresh Whipped Cream (page 265).

This is the iconic Canadian dessert bar turned pie. When it comes down to it, the method is pretty much the same—it's the shape that is different. The base is a pressed chocolate graham coconut crumb crust, and it's topped with sweet, creamy custard icing and finished with rich chocolate ganache. This is one for the holidays.

NANAIMO BAR PIE

MAKES ONE 9-INCH SINGLE-CRUST PIE

1 recipe Nanaimo Bar Crust (page 42)

Custard Layer

½ cup (114 g) butter, softened

3 Tbsp heavy cream

¼ cup (35 g) custard powder

2 cups (280 g) icing sugar

2 Tbsp Baileys Irish Cream

Chocolate Layer

2 cups (340 g) semi-sweet chocolate chips

¼ cup (57 g) butter

Decoration

2 cups (300 g) Whipped Cream (page 265)

1 tsp custard powder (optional)

1. Prepare a single 9-inch Nanaimo Bar Crust. Chill in the pie plate until you're ready to assemble your pie.

2. For the custard layer, using a stand mixer fitted with the paddle attachment, cream the butter, cream, and custard powder until light and fluffy. With the stand mixer running on medium-low speed, add the icing sugar, a bit at a time, mixing until smooth. In a slow and steady stream, add the Baileys and continue to mix until smooth and creamy.

3. Fill the pie shell with the custard and smooth it out to have a nice even top. The pie shell will be about half full. Chill for a minimum of 2 hours.

4. For the chocolate layer, melt the chocolate and butter together in a double boiler over medium heat, or heat in 30-second intervals in the microwave, stirring between each. Stir until well mixed.

5. Pour the chocolate mixture over the chilled pie, spreading it evenly over the pie's surface. Let cool completely.

6. To decorate, using a piping bag fitted with the star tip, pipe whipped cream rosettes over the top of the pie. I like to add 1 tsp of custard powder to the cream just before whipping it to give it that nice yellow color synonymous with a Nanaimo bar.

am dreaming up pie recipes all the time, and as a result, The Pie Hole has quite a few pies that simply do not fit into the standard pie categories. It is through these pies that a lot of my creativity really shines. Sometimes I literally dream the flavors. I'll wake up and run to the bakery, all excited to make a new pie a reality. When one comes together into something truly special, I just can't wait to share it. Likewise with the classics—Lemon Meringue, Key Lime, and Pumpkin—I love my version of these perennial favorites. They're classics for a reason after all!

This is a special pie that we only make for The Pie Hole's birthday on May 26. Is it a cake or is it a pie? This whimsical creation is honestly the best of both worlds with vanilla cake, vanilla buttercream frosting, and white chocolate ganache—not to mention some happy little sprinkles.

BIRTHDAY CAKE PIE

MAKES ONE 9-INCH SINGLE-CRUST PIE

½ recipe Double Butter Crust (page 20)

1 cup (200 g) sugar

½ cup (114 g) butter, at room temperature

2 eggs

2 tsp vanilla

1½ cups (225 g) flour

1¾ tsp baking powder

Pinch salt

½ cup (125 mL) milk

2¾ cups (660 g) Buttercream Frosting (page 270)

2 cups (300 g) Whipped Cream (page 265)

1 drop food coloring (we like Regal Purple from Americolor)

Sprinkles, for garnish

White Chocolate Ganache

⅓ cup (80 mL) heavy cream

1 cup (170 g) white chocolate chips

1 Tbsp unsalted butter

1. Prepare a single 9-inch Double Butter Crust and fully blind bake (page 24). Prepare a 9-inch cake pan by greasing or lining with parchment paper.

2. Using a stand mixer fitted with the paddle attachment, cream the sugar and butter on medium-high speed until fluffy, about 3 minutes. Turn the speed down to medium-low and mix in the eggs. Add the vanilla and mix for another minute, until fully incorporated.

3. Combine the flour, baking powder, and salt. With the mixer running on low, add the dry ingredients, 1 Tbsp at a time. Slowly add the milk and mix well. Pour into the prepared cake pan.

4. Bake the cake for 35 to 40 minutes, until a skewer inserted comes out clean. Let cool.

5. Crumble the cooled cake into a large bowl. It should make about 4½ cups of crumble. Using your hands, mix in 1¼ cups of the buttercream frosting until fully combined.

6. Add the cake filling to the bottom of the pie shell, pressing down on the cake mixture until the shell is filled by half.

7. Add the whipped cream to a medium bowl. Gently fold in ½ cup of buttercream frosting until fully mixed. Spread the fluffy icing whip over the cake layer and smooth to even out the top. Freeze for 20 minutes to set.

8. For the white chocolate ganache, heat the cream until steaming in a small pot over medium heat. Remove from the heat and add the white chocolate and butter. Wait 3 minutes, then stir to combine. Let cool to room temperature.

9. Top the chilled pie with the cooled white chocolate ganache layer and chill to allow it to set.

10. In a medium bowl, add a drop of food coloring to the remaining buttercream and stir to combine. Pipe a rosette border of icing and finish with your favorite sprinkles. Chill in the fridge and remove 20 to 30 minutes before serving.

This pie was born out of a dare to put bacon in a dessert pie. I never back down from a challenge. Bacon, often known as the savory and salty accompaniment to breakfast, felt like the perfect addition to a French toast pie. The bread-like texture comes from lightly spiced white cake, the egg comes from maple custard, which infuses in the cake, and we top it off with a bacon golden sugar crumble. I personally don't think you need an excuse to eat pie for breakfast, but if you do this pie checks all the right boxes.

MAPLE FRENCH TOAST BACON PIE

MAKES ONE 9-INCH SINGLE-CRUST PIE

½ recipe Double Butter Crust
    (page 20)

Cake "Toast" Layer

1 cup (200 g) sugar

½ cup (114 g) butter,
    at room temperature

2 eggs

2 tsp vanilla

1½ cups (225 g) flour

1¾ tsp baking powder

½ tsp cinnamon

½ tsp nutmeg

Pinch salt

½ cup (125 mL) milk

1. Prepare a single 9-inch Double Butter Crust and partially blind bake (page 24). Chill the dough until you're ready to assemble your pie. Line a baking sheet with parchment paper.

2. For the cake "toast" layer, using a stand mixer fitted with the paddle attachment, cream the sugar and butter on medium-high speed until nice and fluffy, about 3 minutes.

3. Turn the speed down to medium-low and add the eggs 1 at a time, beating for 30 seconds between each egg. Add the vanilla and mix for 1 minute, until the mixture is fully incorporated.

4. In a medium bowl, combine the flour, baking powder, cinnamon, nutmeg, and salt. With the stand mixer running on low speed, mix in the dry ingredients, 1 Tbsp at a time. In a slow and steady stream, add the milk and mix well.

Maple Custard "Egg" Layer

⅓ cup (66 g) golden sugar

1 Tbsp white cornmeal

2 tsp flour

½ tsp salt

1 Tbsp butter, melted

1 tsp vanilla

1 cup (250 mL) sour cream

3 eggs

1 egg yolk

1 cup (250 mL) maple syrup

3 cups (450 g) Bacon Golden
        Sugar Crumble (page 251)

5. For the maple custard "egg" layer, using a stand mixer fitted with the paddle attachment, combine the golden sugar, white cornmeal, flour, salt, and butter. Add the vanilla and sour cream and stir until smooth. Add the eggs and egg yolk, 1 at a time, stirring between each. Add the maple syrup and mix until very smooth. If the mixture has any lumps, use a fine-mesh sieve to strain them out.

6. Fill the prepared pie shell one-quarter full with the cake "toast" layer and smooth it out to have a nice even top. Pour the maple custard "egg" layer overtop until the pie is three-quarters full.

7. Preheat the oven to 350°F. Transfer the pie to the prepared baking sheet.

8. Bake for 35 minutes, until mostly firm with a slight jiggle in the middle. Remove from the oven and top with the bacon golden sugar crumble. Bake for an additional 15 minutes. Let cool completely. This pie can be served at room temperature or warmed up and drizzled with a little maple syrup. . . yum!

Happy birthday to me! My favorite birthday cake has always been a Black Forest cake, so it was a no-brainer to create a Black Forest pie. I match the flavor with rich chocolate and sour cherry compote spiked with kirsch, finished with a whipped cream spiked with kirsch.

BLACK FOREST PIE

MAKES ONE 9-INCH SINGLE-CRUST PIE

½ recipe Dark Chocolate Crumb Crust (page 41)

¾ cup (175 mL) heavy cream

⅓ cup (80 mL) milk

2 eggs

1½ cups (255 g) semi-sweet chocolate chips

¼ cup (50 g) sugar

Pinch salt

1 batch Sour Cherry Compote (page 262)

⅓ batch Kirsch Whipped Cream (page 266)

¼ cup (20 g) dark chocolate curls or shards

1. Prepare a single 9-inch Dark Chocolate Crumb Crust and partially blind bake. Chill until you're ready to assemble your pie. Line a baking sheet with parchment paper.

2. In a large saucepan over medium heat, bring the cream and milk to a simmer.

3. While the mixture is getting hot, in a medium bowl, whisk the eggs until very smooth.

4. Once the milk is hot, add the chocolate chips and stir until completely melted. Whisk in the sugar and salt, and mix well to dissolve.

5. Carefully, in a slow and steady stream, pour about half of the hot chocolate mixture into the eggs, whisking constantly, to temper the eggs. Tempering gently brings the eggs to a higher temperature without cooking them and making them lumpy. If you do get some lumps, you can use a fine-mesh sieve to remove them. Return the mixture to the pot, and mix until combined. There is no need to bring to a boil; the filling will bake and set in the oven.

6. Pour the chocolate mixture into the prepared chocolate crumb shell until full. Bake for 25 minutes, or until the filling is set with little jiggle and the surface has gone from glossy to matte. Let cool for a minimum of 4 hours to overnight before decorating.

7. Top the cooled pie with the sour cherry compote. Smooth to an even layer, focusing on the center of the pie, as a ring of kirsch whipped cream is added next.

8. Using a piping bag fitted with the star tip, pipe the kirsch whipped cream rosettes around the outer edges of the pie. Sprinkle with dark chocolate curls. Serve chilled.

I used to make mini versions of these pies to bring camping, where I would gently warm them on a grill over the campfire. Such delicious memories. This pie has everything to satisfy your summer cravings: thick graham crumb crust, creamy chocolate filling, and a marshmallow meringue all toasted up. Sorry, no campfire included.

S'MORE PIE

MAKES ONE 9-INCH SINGLE-CRUST PIE

1 recipe Graham Cracker Crust (page 36)

Chocolate Layer

⅓ cup (80 mL) heavy cream

3 Tbsp milk

1 egg

¾ cup (130 g) semi-sweet chocolate chips

2 Tbsp sugar

Pinch salt

Marshmallow Layer

2¾ cups (165 g) mini marshmallows

½ cup (125 mL) milk

1½ cups (375 mL) heavy cream

1½ tsp vanilla

1 batch Italian Meringue (page 268)

1. Prepare a single 9-inch Graham Cracker Crust and partially blind bake (page 24). Chill in the pie plate until you're ready to assemble your pie. Preheat the oven to 350°F.

2. For the chocolate layer, in a large saucepan, combine the cream and milk and set over medium heat.

3. While the mixture is getting hot, in a medium bowl, whisk the egg until very smooth.

4. Once the milk is steaming hot (not boiling), remove from the heat, add the chocolate chips, and stir until completely melted. Whisk in the sugar and salt and mix well to dissolve.

5. Carefully, in a slow and steady stream, pour ⅓ cup of the chocolate mixture into the egg, while vigorously whisking, to temper the egg. Tempering gently brings the egg to a higher temperature without cooking it and making it lumpy. If you do get some lumps, you can use a fine-mesh sieve to remove them. Add the tempered mixture back to the saucepan.

6. Fill the pie shell half full with the chocolate mixture. Bake for 10 to 12 minutes, until the filling is set and does not jiggle with a gentle shake. Let cool completely.

7. For the marshmallow layer, in a large saucepan over low heat, combine the mini marshmallows and milk. Cook until the mixture begins to foam (not boil) then remove from the heat and stir until the marshmallows are completely melted and the mixture is smooth. Add the vanilla and stir. Set aside at room temperature to allow the mixture to begin to cool, stirring often to keep the cooling even. Do not allow the mixture to cool completely, or the gelatin will re-set and this layer will be lumpy.

8. Using a stand mixer fitted with the whisk attachment, whisk the cream at medium-low speed until soft peaks form. Gently fold in the marshmallow mixture with a spatula and mix well.

9. Add the marshmallow mixture on top of the chocolate layer of the pie and chill for at least 2 hours to allow it to set.

10. Using a piping bag fitted with a big round tip, pipe the Italian meringue over the top of the entire pie. The meringue should have a billowy soft-serve ice cream look. Use a kitchen torch to carefully brown the meringue. (Because of the middle layer, this pie cannot go into the oven to brown the meringue.) Serve at room temperature.

hen I introduced the name of this pie to my staff of young twentysomethings, no one had a clue who Magnum P.I. was. When I showed them a photo, a few people recognized him as Monica's boyfriend on *Friends*. I felt old. Nonetheless this tropical pie full of coconut, chocolate, caramel, and shortbread cookies is delicious, and it's named after Magnum and his Hawaiian shirts.

MAGNUM P.I.(E)

MAKES ONE 9-INCH SINGLE-CRUST PIE

½ recipe Dark Chocolate Crumb Crust (page 41)

Shortbread Cookies

1 cup (227 g) butter

½ cup (70 g) icing sugar

¼ cup (32 g) cornstarch

1½ cups (225 g) flour

¼ tsp salt

1¼ tsp vanilla

1 cup (170 g) chocolate chips

3 Tbsp butter, at room temperature

¼ cup (50 g) sugar

¼ cup (60 mL) golden corn syrup

¼ cup (60 mL) sweetened condensed milk

1 cup (180 g) Toasted Coconut (page 254)

1. Prepare a single 9-inch Dark Chocolate Crumb Crust and fully blind bake. Chill until you're ready to assemble your pie.

2. For the shortbread cookies, using a stand mixer fitted with the paddle attachment, cream the butter and sugar on medium-low speed until fluffy. Add the cornstarch, flour, and salt and mix on low speed until combined. Add 1 tsp of the vanilla and mix on high speed until fluffy, 2 to 3 minutes. Wrap the cookie dough tightly in plastic wrap and chill for 30 minutes.

3. Preheat the oven to 350°F. Line a baking sheet with parchment paper.

4. On a floured surface using a rolling pin, roll out the dough until it is ¼ inch thick. Cut out 2-inch round cookies, making as many cookies as you can (about 24), and spread out evenly 1 inch apart on the prepared baking sheet. Chill for 15 minutes, then bake for 12 to 15 minutes. The cookies should just start to brown at the bottom edges. Let cool.

5. Line a cupcake pan with 12 silicone cupcake liners or use a nonstick cupcake pan.

6. Melt the chocolate in a microwave-safe dish for 30 seconds and give it a stir. Continue to microwave at 15-second intervals, stirring between each interval until fully melted. Place 2 Tbsp of the melted chocolate in the bottom of each cupcake liner.

7. Gently press a cookie into the chocolate lining of each cup. Reserve the rest of the cookies for the pie filling.

Filling

1 cup (227 g) softened cream
  cheese

¼ cup (50 g) sugar

⅓ cup (80 mL) Caramel Sauce
  (page 258)

1 tsp vanilla

½ cup (125 mL) heavy cream

¼ cup (45 g) Toasted Coconut
  (page 254)

2 Tbsp Chocolate Ganache
  (page 261)

2 Tbsp Caramel Sauce (page 258)

½ cup (75 g) Whipped Cream
  (page 265)

4 Samoa cookies, quartered

8. In a medium saucepan over medium heat, combine the butter, sugar, corn syrup, condensed milk, and the remaining ¼ tsp of vanilla. With a spatula, stir until the butter has melted and has a smooth consistency. Remove from the heat and add the toasted coconut. Stir to evenly coat the coconut. The mixture will be thick. Divide the mixture evenly among the cupcake liners, filling to cover each cookie. Smooth out the top by pressing the mixture down. Set aside at room temperature to set.

9. Carefully remove the cupcake liners or use an offset spatula or butter knife to gently slide down the sides of the cookies to pop them out of the pan.

10. For the filling, using a stand mixer fitted with the paddle attachment or a hand mixer in a large bowl, combine the cream cheese, sugar, caramel sauce, and vanilla on medium speed until completely smooth. Transfer to another bowl if using a stand mixer.

11. Using the same stand mixer or a hand mixer in another large bowl, whip the cream on medium speed to achieve soft peaks. Using a spatula, gently fold in the caramel cream cheese mixture until fully combined. Add the toasted coconut. Crush 12 of the shortbread cookies and fold the cookie crumbs into the mixture.

12. Fill the bottom shell with the cream cheese mixture and smooth it out to have a nice even top. Drizzle with the chocolate ganache and caramel sauce. Using a piping bag fitted with a round tip, pipe the whipped cream around the edge of the pie. Chill for a minimum of 4 hours before serving. When ready to serve, evenly space the shortbread cookie quarters in the whipped cream.

This pie has become a favorite with a lot of our regular customers. With a thick sweetened condensed milk custard over a graham cracker crust, a layer of espresso-spiked whipped cream, and little chevrons of chocolate ganache to finish, this pie is a coffee lover's dream.

VIETNAMESE COFFEE PIE

MAKES ONE 9-INCH SINGLE-CRUST PIE

1 recipe Graham Cracker Crust (page 36)

One 14 oz (398 mL) can sweetened condensed milk

1 egg

1 Tbsp lime juice

¼ cup (60 mL) espresso

2 cups (300 g) Espresso Coffee Whipped Cream (page 266)

1 Tbsp Chocolate Ganache (page 261), warmed

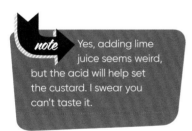

note Yes, adding lime juice seems weird, but the acid will help set the custard. I swear you can't taste it.

1. Preheat the oven to 350°F. Prepare a single 9-inch Graham Cracker Crust and partially blind bake. Chill until you're ready to assemble your pie. Line a baking sheet with parchment paper.

2. In a large bowl, combine the condensed milk, egg, lime juice, and espresso. Using an eggbeater or whisk, slowly and carefully mix. Take it slow, as the espresso and lime juice will float on top of the much heavier condensed milk and can splash everywhere.

3. To assemble the pie, fill the pie shell with the coffee custard filling. Place the pie on the prepared baking sheet and carefully transfer the pie to the oven. This filling is quite runny before baking, so steady hands are required.

4. Bake for 15 to 20 minutes, until the edges are set and the center has a tiny jiggle with a gentle shake. Let cool completely in the fridge.

5. To decorate, add 1½ cups of the espresso whipped cream and smooth as much as possible to have a nice even top. Carefully drizzle the chocolate ganache in 5 to 8 perpendicular lines as straight as possible across the pie. Working quickly, turn the pie 90 degrees and softly drag a paring knife through the lines to create a chevron pattern. Move over ½ to ¾ inch and drag the knife in the opposite direction. Continue to alternate until you have done the whole pie top.

6. Using a piping bag with a round tip, pipe the remaining espresso whipped cream around the outer edge of the pie.

7. Let the pie chill for 1 hour minimum before serving.

woke up one morning with the sun shining brightly, and I couldn't get the idea of pink lemonade out of my head. I called my head chef and told her that we would launch a whole pink lemonade summer series: pie, pop tarts (page 232), and a refreshing drink. I went in and baked up what I was envisioning, and with one bite I was in heaven. It was everything I hoped for and more—a pretty and flirty summer pie.

PINK LEMONADE PIE

MAKES ONE 9-INCH SINGLE-CRUST PIE

½ recipe Double Butter Crust (page 20)

1½ cups (300 g) sugar

⅓ cup (42 g) cornstarch

¾ cup (175 mL) lemon juice

1½ Tbsp lemon zest

5 egg yolks, beaten

1½ cups (375 mL) milk

¼ cup (57 g) butter

1 batch Raspberry Compote (page 262)

1 batch Pretty in Pink Meringue (page 268)

1. Prepare a single 9-inch Double Butter Crust and fully blind bake (page 24). Chill until you're ready to assemble your pie.

2. To make the lemon layer, in a large pot, combine the sugar, cornstarch, lemon juice, lemon zest, egg yolks, and milk and whisk to fully mix. Cook over medium heat, stirring continuously, until the mixture thickens. Once it begins to boil, stir for another 30 seconds. Remove from the heat and add the butter. Stir until the butter is melted and fully mixed in.

3. To assemble the pie, take the pie shell and fill the bottom with the raspberry compote. Carefully pour the lemon mixture over the raspberry layer, trying not to mix the 2 layers. Lightly press a piece of plastic wrap on the surface and chill for at least 4 hours or overnight for the pie to set.

4. When the pie is chilled, top with the Pretty in Pink Meringue. Top the pie nice and high but make sure to cover the entire surface, pushing the meringue right to the edge of the pie crust.

I am always asked the big question: What is your favorite pie? The answer used to vary depending on my mood, the season, or even who I was talking to. Until one day, while stuffing not one but several mini lemon meringues in my mouth, I realized my favorite truly is the Lemon Meringue Pie. With all my crazy creations, I know it might seem like a safe pick, but who cares—you should always follow your heart and tummy!

LEMON MERINGUE PIE

MAKES ONE 9-INCH SINGLE-CRUST PIE

½ recipe Double Butter Crust (page 20)

1½ cups (300 g) sugar

⅓ cup (42 g) cornstarch

¾ cup (175 mL) lemon juice

1½ Tbsp lemon zest

5 egg yolks, beaten

1½ cups (375 mL) milk

¼ cup (57 g) butter

1 batch Italian Meringue (page 268)

1. Prepare a single 9-inch Double Butter Crust and fully blind bake (page 24). Chill until you're ready to assemble your pie.

2. In a large pot, combine the sugar, cornstarch, lemon juice, lemon zest, egg yolks, and milk and whisk to fully combine. Cook over medium heat, stirring continuously, until the mixture thickens. Once it begins to boil, stir for another 30 seconds. Remove from the heat and add the butter. Stir until the butter is melted and fully mixed in.

3. To assemble the pie, add the hot lemon mixture to the pie shell and smooth it out to have a nice even top. Lightly press a piece of plastic wrap on the surface and chill for at least 4 hours or overnight to allow it to set.

4. When the pie is chilled, top with the Italian meringue. Top the pie nice and high but make sure to cover the entire surface, pushing the meringue right to the edge of the pie crust. This helps protect the delicate filling when you torch the meringue.

5. Use a kitchen torch to carefully brown the meringue, or place the pie on a parchment-lined baking sheet on the bottom rack of your oven and broil for 3 to 4 minutes. Keep a very close eye on the pie, as it doesn't take long to burn the meringue.

The name "key lime pie" just rolls off the tongue, but you won't want that happening when you eat this easy and delicious pie. With the tartness of the lime and the creaminess of the custard all balanced with fresh whipped cream and lightly toasted graham cracker crust, you will make sure every last morsel makes it into your pie hole.

KEY LIME PIE

MAKES ONE 9-INCH SINGLE-CRUST PIE

1 recipe Graham Cracker Crust (page 36)

Two 28 oz (798 mL) cans sweetened condensed milk

2 eggs

1 cup (250 mL) lime juice or key lime juice (see Note)

2 tsp lime zest

2 cups (300 g) Whipped Cream (page 265)

Fresh key lime slices (optional)

note Key lime juice is a specialty item not easily found. Moreover, trying to juice tiny key limes is terribly hard! Once I squeezed enough for 4 whole cups . . . and then knocked it over. Still haunts me. Anyway, regular lime juice does work nicely in its place.

1. Prepare a single 9-inch Graham Cracker Crust and partially blind bake (page 24). Chill until you're ready to assemble your pie. Preheat the oven to 350°F. Line a baking sheet with parchment paper.

2. In a large bowl, combine the condensed milk, eggs, lime juice, and 1 tsp of the lime zest. As the condensed milk is heavy and the lime juice floats on the surface, it can splash around, so whisk very carefully until the juice works its way in. Continue to mix until smooth and creamy.

3. Add the lime mixture to the pie shell and smooth it out to have a nice even top. Bake on the baking sheet for 15 to 20 minutes, until the top does not jiggle and has a matte sheen. Let cool completely in the fridge.

4. To decorate, fit a piping bag with the star tip and fill with the fresh whipped cream. Pipe a full ring of fluffy rosettes around the pie and position fresh key slices on top, if using. Finish by sprinkling the remaining 1 tsp of lime zest onto the piped rosettes. Serve chilled.

This was my first attempt ever at making a vegan pie, and it was such a hit. Sadly, it doesn't show up on our menu for two very good reasons, and both involve the avocados. First, the avocado browns quickly and while it doesn't change the delicious flavor, as the saying goes, we eat with our eyes first. Second, any time someone would order this pie, I wouldn't be able to find a ripe avocado to save my life, let alone five of them.

VEGAN AVOCADO KEY LIME PIE

MAKES ONE 9-INCH SINGLE-CRUST PIE

1 recipe Vegan Coconut Walnut Crust (page 38)

5 large, ripe avocados

½ cup (125 mL) lime juice

⅓ cup (80 mL) maple syrup

1½ tsp lime zest

1½ Tbsp coconut oil

2 drops coconut emulsion (optional)

1 Tbsp shredded coconut or 2 cups (300 g) Vegan Coconut Whip (page 267)

¼ cup (45 g) Toasted Coconut (page 254) (optional)

1. Prepare a single 9-inch Vegan Coconut Walnut Crust. Chill until you're ready to assemble your pie.

2. In a food processor, blend the avocados until they have broken down. Add the lime juice and maple syrup and blend until creamy. Add the lime zest, coconut oil, and coconut emulsion, if using. Mix for another 30 seconds to 1 minute, until the mixture is super smooth.

3. Add the avocado mixture to the pie shell and smooth it out to have a nice even top. Top with the coconut. Store in the freezer and bring to room temperature before eating.

4. You can alternatively top with coconut whip and, if you are not on a raw diet, toasted coconut. If you use the coconut whip, eat right away and do not freeze the pie.

5. To serve, remove from the freezer 15 to 20 minutes before serving. This pie is delicious super cold!

No table is complete during the holidays without a pumpkin pie. But why reserve this pie for the holidays when during the fall and winter months a nice slice of pumpkin pie is good any day of the week? Whether you like your slice straight up or with whipped cream, just make sure you save room for this dessert.

PUMPKIN PIE

MAKES ONE 9-INCH SINGLE-CRUST PIE

½ recipe Double Butter Crust (page 20)

⅓ cup (76 g) butter, at room temperature

1 cup (200 g) golden sugar

2 cups (500 g) pumpkin puree

⅓ cup (42 g) cornstarch

2 tsp cinnamon

1 tsp nutmeg

¼ tsp salt

½ cup (125 mL) full-fat sour cream

½ tsp ground ginger

3 eggs

¾ cup (175 mL) milk

2 tsp vanilla

2 cups (300 g) Whipped Cream (page 265) (optional)

1. Prepare a single 9-inch Double Butter Crust. Chill the dough in the pie plate until you're ready to assemble your pie. Line a baking sheet with parchment paper.

2. Using a stand mixer fitted with the paddle attachment, cream the butter until light and fluffy. Add the golden sugar and the pumpkin puree and continue mixing on medium speed, scraping down the sides at least once.

3. Add the cornstarch, cinnamon, nutmeg, salt, sour cream, and ginger and continue to mix on medium-low speed. Add the eggs and mix well for 30 to 45 seconds, until combined. Add the milk and vanilla and mix for 1 to 2 minutes, until nice and smooth.

4. Add the pumpkin mixture to the pie shell and smooth it out to have a nice even top. Preheat the oven to 350°F. Chill the pie for 30 minutes in the fridge or 15 minutes in the freezer before baking. Transfer the pie to the prepared baking sheet.

5. Bake for 45 to 50 minutes, until the center is just a bit jiggly and the edges of the pumpkin filling are set. Let the pie cool to room temperature before serving.

6. If desired, serve with a bowl of whipped cream on the side for self serve or use a piping bag fitted with the star tip to pipe whipped cream rosettes around the edge of the pie and finish with a little pinch of nutmeg sprinkled over the whipped cream.

By popular demand for Thanksgiving, we created this undeniably delicious vegan version of the pumpkin pie. No one would ever guess there is tofu hiding in the filling, as it is the pumpkin and beautiful spices that shine through. Use our Vegan Coconut Whip (page 267) and fresh grated nutmeg to finish the pie.

VEGAN PUMPKIN PIE

MAKES ONE 9-INCH SINGLE-CRUST PIE

½ recipe Vegan Pie Crust (page 25)

1½ cups (339 g) silken tofu

2 cups (500 g) pumpkin puree

1¼ cups (250 g) organic cane sugar

2 Tbsp cornstarch

½ Tbsp cinnamon

½ tsp ground ginger

1 tsp nutmeg, plus extra for garnish

Pinch salt

1 tsp vanilla

2 cups (300 g) Vegan Coconut Whip (page 267)

1. Preheat oven to 350°F. Prepare a single 9-inch Vegan Pie Crust and partially blind bake (page 24). Chill in the pie plate until you're ready to assemble your pie. Line a baking sheet with parchment paper.

2. In a food processor, blend the tofu on high speed for 30 seconds to 1 minute until smooth and creamy. Add the pumpkin puree and blend for 30 seconds.

3. Add the sugar, cornstarch, cinnamon, ginger, nutmeg, salt, and vanilla and blend on high speed for 1 to 2 minutes until creamy, scraping down the sides as needed.

4. Add the pumpkin mixture to the pie shell and smooth it out to make a nice even top. Bake for 30 to 35 minutes, until the edges are set and the middle of the pie does not jiggle too much with a gentle shake. The pie will continue to cook a little as it begins to cool. Cool completely.

5. To decorate, top with a mound of coconut whip and grate nutmeg overtop. Enjoy this pie at room temperature.

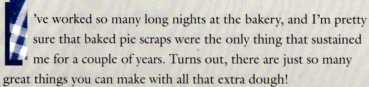

I've worked so many long nights at the bakery, and I'm pretty sure that baked pie scraps were the only thing that sustained me for a couple of years. Turns out, there are just so many great things you can make with all that extra dough!

The recipes in this chapter are very flexible. The yields of the recipes show how much can be made from a full batch of dough but you can use however much leftover dough you have on hand, and scale up or down with toppings as you like. I've suggested using Double Butter Crust dough (page 20) throughout, but the Vegan Pie Crust dough (page 25) works just fine, too.

Whenever you have leftover dough scraps, just form them into a little disk without working them too much, then chill for 20 to 30 minutes before using. If you don't have enough left from one pie, you can always wrap your scraps securely and freeze them, adding more as you get them. Once you have enough, defrost the dough in the fridge before rolling it out to use. *Tip: The more you work pie dough, the tougher it gets. Make sure to only roll it out a maximum of three times.*

hether pasties, calzones, pierogis, empanadas, Jamaican patties, or samosas, many cultures have their own version of the handpie. There is just something about taking a dough round, filling it, and biting into a pocket of goodness. Handpies are so convenient to have on the go and are the absolute perfect size for lunch (see the photos on pages 77 and 78). While we only make ours with savory fillings (and any of the savory pie fillings in this book will work well), you can definitely make sweet versions, too.

The consistency of your fillings is important for handpies. Soupy fillings will not work! Savory fillings need to be cold to work with, and fruit fillings work best when they are chilled and thick. I like to add a topping to my handpies: rosemary, cracked pepper, thyme, paprika, grated cheese, or parmesan for savory pies, and a sprinkling of sugar or cinnamon sugar for fruit pies. If you are making a few different flavors, having a topping or some other kind of marking will help you tell them apart.

HANDPIES

MAKES EIGHT HANDPIES OR TWENTY-FOUR MINI HANDPIES

1 batch Double Butter Dough (page 20)

Egg Wash (page 43)

4 cups your choice of filling (see above)

note You can freeze unbaked handpies to bake later. Lay the unbaked handpies flat on a parchment-lined baking sheet and place them in the freezer. Once they are frozen through, stack them in a freezer bag and seal with as little air as possible. These will keep for up to 3 months in the freezer. When ready to bake, preheat the oven to 350°F and place the frozen handpies on a parchment-lined baking sheet. Bake for 45 minutes or until golden brown.

1. Prepare the dough (or collect the dough scraps) and chill in the fridge until you're ready to use it. If your dough is frozen, fully thaw it first. Line a baking sheet with parchment paper.

2. Sprinkle your work surface with flour and use a rolling pin to start rolling out the dough. Rotate the dough 90 degrees after every few passes to work toward creating a circular shape. If the circumference of the disk is not getting larger as you roll, there's a good chance the dough is stuck to the surface below. Carefully lift the dough and add more flour to the surface. Continue rolling until the dough is about ¼ inch thick.

3. Place a bowl 7 inches in diameter for regular handpies or 4 inches in diameter for mini handpies over the dough. Use the bowl as a template to cut 8 large or 24 small perfect circles.

4. Place the rounds evenly spaced on the prepared baking sheet. Brush half of each round's surface with egg wash. Evenly divide your filling between the handpies and place some filling in the center of each round. Fold the round in half and use the back of a fork or your fingers to secure the edges and seal the handpie. Brush the whole surface with egg wash. Cut three little ½-inch slits to vent the handpie. Preheat the oven to 350°F. Chill the handpies for 30 minutes in the fridge or 15 minutes in the freezer before baking.

5. Bake for 35 to 40 minutes, until golden brown.

t doesn't get better than pop tarts, especially as these homemade versions taste so much better and bring all the whimsy with pink icing and sprinkles. When we have these on the counter at the shops, you can see the twinkles in customers' eyes, no matter their age. Talk about nostalgic childhood memories. This recipe is for PB&J pop tarts, but we make a huge variety of flavors with different icing-glazed tops for each. See page 232 for some other variation ideas, or feel free to swap in 3 Tbsp of any of the fruit pie fillings!

PB&J POP TARTS

MAKES 8 POP TARTS

1 batch Double Butter Crust dough (page 20)

½ batch Raspberry Compote (page 262), room temperature

Egg Wash (page 43)

Peanut Butter Filling

½ cup (125 g) smooth peanut butter

2 Tbsp unsalted butter, softened

3 Tbsp icing sugar

1 tsp vanilla

Peanut Butter Icing

2 Tbsp milk

2 Tbsp smooth peanut butter

⅔ cup (93 g) icing sugar

½ tsp vanilla

note If you are preparing these in advance, place the unbaked pop tarts in an airtight container and freeze for up to 3 months.

1. Prepare the dough (or collect the dough scraps) and chill in the fridge until you're ready to use it. If your dough is frozen, fully thaw it first.

2. Sprinkle your work surface with flour. Use a rolling pin to start rolling out the dough into a rectangular shape. If the disk is not getting larger as you roll, there's a good chance the dough is stuck to the surface below. Carefully lift the dough and add more flour to the surface. Continue rolling until you have a rough 12-by-20-inch rectangle and the dough is about ⅛ inch thick. Cut the dough into sixteen 3-by-5-inch rectangles. Keep them refrigerated on a parchment-lined baking sheet until you're ready to assemble the pop tarts.

3. For the peanut butter filling, in a stand mixer fitted with the paddle attachment, cream the peanut butter and butter on medium speed until combined. With the mixer running on low speed, add the icing sugar and continue mixing to fully incorporate. Add the vanilla and mix well. This filling can be refrigerated in an airtight container for 1 week.

4. To assemble the pop tarts, preheat the oven to 350°F. Line a baking sheet with parchment paper. Place 8 dough rectangles 2 inches apart on the prepared baking sheet. Brush the edges of the rectangles with egg wash.

5. Take 2 piping bags or plastic bags with a corner snipped off, and fill 1 with the raspberry compote and the other with the peanut butter filling. Pipe or spread 1 line of raspberry and 1 line of

Pink Icing

¼ cup (35 g) icing sugar

1 tsp milk

1 drop red food coloring
(or your favorite color)

peanut butter in the center of the pop tart. Cover each with another rectangle of dough, and use the back of a fork or your fingers to secure the edges around. Brush the whole surface with egg wash. Cut three ½-inch slits in the center to vent the pop tart.

6. Bake for 20 to 25 minutes, or until golden brown. Remove from the oven and allow to cool completely.

7. For the peanut butter icing, in a small bowl, mix together the milk, peanut butter, icing sugar, and vanilla. Carefully spread the icing onto the cooled pop tarts. Don't go too close to the edges, as the icing will run a little until it sets.

8. For the pink icing, in a separate small bowl, mix the icing sugar and milk. Dip a toothpick into the food coloring and stir it into the icing. Repeat with a fresh toothpick until you get a pink color that will contrast nicely with the peanut butter icing.

9. Using a piping bag or plastic bag with a corner snipped, pipe a thin wavy line over the surface of the pop tart. Allow the icing to set, then take a bite and feel like you are back in kindergarten.

Variations

STRAWBERRY RHUBARB

Substitute 3 Tbsp of Strawberry Rhubarb Compote (page 262) instead of the raspberry. I love these with a double batch of Pink Icing (see above) and classic sprinkles.

SOUR CHERRY

Substitute 3 Tbsp of Sour Cherry Compote (page 262) instead of the raspberry. Try a pink icing with a purple icing squiggle across the top for these (see Pink Icing, above).

PINK LEMONADE

Add 3 Tbsp of the filling for Pink Lemonade Pie (page 214) to each rectangle. Decorate with the icing of your choice or even pretty pink meringue.

mean, what goes better with pie than ice cream? So, why aren't ice cream and pie filling sandwiched between buttery flaky pie crust more of a thing? I started turning all of my sweet pies into amazing "P"ice cream sammies, as I called them, and sold them at farmers' markets over the summer and OMG . . . they are next level! While you can try so many different flavors, the one that was most popular for us was the Fat Elvis (see page 235).

"P"ICE CREAM SANDWICH

MAKES 8 SANDWICHES

No-Churn Ice Cream

2 oz (57 g) cream cheese, softened

2 cups (500 mL) heavy cream

One 14 oz (398 mL) can sweetened condensed milk

1 tsp vanilla

Pinch salt

Pie Crust Cookies

1 batch Double Butter Crust dough (page 20)

¼ cup (50 g) sugar

Egg Wash (page 43)

½ cup (125 mL) desired filling (page 262) (optional)

1. For the no-churn ice cream, using a stand mixer fitted with the whisk attachment, beat the cream cheese on medium-high speed until very smooth. Turn the mixer speed to low and slowly add the cream to incorporate, then turn the speed to high. Whip until stiff peaks form.

2. In a separate bowl, use a whisk to mix the condensed milk, vanilla, and salt until thoroughly combined. Gently fold half the whipped cream mixture into the condensed milk mixture to combine. Add the condensed milk mixture to the remaining whipped cream and beat on a very low speed until just combined and smooth.

3. Line a loaf pan with parchment paper. Add the whipped cream mixture. Chill in the freezer for at least 8 hours, but preferably overnight.

4. For the pie crust cookies, prepare the dough (or collect the dough scraps) and chill in the fridge until you're ready to use it. If your dough is frozen, fully thaw it first. Preheat the oven to 350°F. Line a baking sheet with parchment paper.

5. Sprinkle your work surface with flour, and use a rolling pin to start rolling half of the disk of dough. Rotate the dough 90 degrees after every few passes to work toward creating a circular shape. If the circumference of the disk is not getting larger as you roll, there's a good chance the dough is stuck to the surface below. Carefully lift the dough and add more flour to the surface. Continue rolling until the dough is about ⅛ inch thick. Use a 3½- to 4-inch cookie cutter to cut out 16 rounds.

Fat Elvis
(opposite)

Strawberry Rhubarb
(page 236)

Key Lime Sammie
(page 236)

Blueberry Goat Cheese Basil
(page 236)

6. Sprinkle a thin, even layer of sugar over the prepared baking sheet. Lay the rounds on top. The sugar will caramelize the bottoms of each pie crust round when baking, which creates a barrier to stop the pastry becoming soggy when you add the ice cream. Brush the surface of each round with egg wash and sprinkle a little more sugar over them.

7. Bake for 15 to 17 minutes, or until golden brown. Let cool completely.

8. To assemble, line a baking sheet with parchment paper. Transfer 8 pie crust rounds to this tray, sugar side up.

9. Let the ice cream soften a touch, then take a generous scoop of ice cream and place it in the center of 1 of the baked pie crust rounds. Use the back of the ice cream scoop to press a little well into the ice cream. If you like, add 1 Tbsp of filling to the well. Top with another pie crust round (sugar side down) and gently squeeze the top and bottom pie crust circles together to form a sandwich. Chill on the baking sheet in the freezer for at least 1 hour.

10. Wrap each sandwich individually in parchment paper and keep frozen.

Variations

FAT ELVIS

As above plus:

1 banana, chopped

⅓ cup (85 g) smooth peanut butter, warmed

⅓ cup (87 g) Chocolate Ganache (page 261)

½ cup (125 mL) Caramel Sauce (page 258)

1 cup (170 g) semi-sweet chocolate chips

3 Tbsp coconut oil

1 cup (140 g) chopped roasted salted peanuts

1. Toss in the chopped banana at the end of step 2 of making the ice cream. In step 3, half fill the loaf pan with the whipped banana ice cream mixture, then drizzle with half of the warmed peanut butter and half of the chocolate ganache. Use the end of a butter knife to swirl the peanut butter and chocolate around a little. Top with the remaining whipped banana cream mixture and drizzle with the rest of the chocolate and peanut butter. Use the same knife to swirl it around a little again.

2. In step 9, fill the well with the caramel sauce.

3. In a microwave-safe bowl, combine the chocolate chips and coconut oil. Melt in 20-second intervals, stirring between each, until the mixture is completely melted, smooth, and creamy.

4. Dip half of the chilled sandwich into the chocolate mixture. Then, working quickly, sprinkle with the chopped roasted salted peanuts. Lay on the prepared baking sheet and chill in the freezer for at least 1 hour.

Variations continued

BLUEBERRY GOAT CHEESE BASIL

As above plus:

2 Tbsp fresh chopped basil

2 oz (57 g) goat cheese
(substitute for cream cheese)

½ cup (125 mL) Blueberry Compote
(page 262)

1. Before starting the no-churn ice cream, in a saucepan over medium-low heat, first combine 2 cups of the cream with the basil and simmer for 5 to 7 minutes. Do not boil. Remove from the heat and chill until cold, at least 2 hours. Start making the no-churn ice cream, substituting goat cheese for the cream cheese in step 1, and using the basil-infused cream.

2. In step 9, fill the well with Blueberry Compote.

KEY LIME SAMMIE

As above plus:

2 Tbsp lime juice

1 Tbsp lime zest

2 cups (340 g) white chocolate
chips

⅓ cup (80 mL) coconut oil

½ cup (65 g) honey graham crumbs

1. In step 2, add the lime juice and the zest.

2. In step 9, no extra filling is needed.

3. In a microwave-safe bowl, combine the white chocolate chips and coconut oil. Melt in 30-second intervals, stirring between each, until the mixture is melted, smooth, and creamy.

4. Dip half of the chilled sandwich into the white chocolate mixture. Then, working quickly, sprinkle it with graham crumbs. Lay on the prepared baking sheet and chill in the freezer for at least 2 hours or overnight.

STRAWBERRY RHUBARB

As above plus:

1 vanilla bean, cut lengthwise
with seeds scraped, or
1 tsp vanilla paste

½ cup (125 mL) Strawberry
Rhubarb Compote (page 262)

1. In step 2 of making the ice cream, substitute the vanilla bean pod or vanilla paste for the vanilla extract.

2. In step 9, fill the well with Strawberry Rhubarb Compote.

I tried to call these "pie-miers," a cheesey take on the French pastry *palmier*, but it didn't quite take. So, cinnamon pie scrolls it is. I love the flaky pastry, and the sugar adds a nice crunch. You don't have to use cinnamon, as a traditional palmier doesn't, but this is not a traditional palmier, so I say pile it on!

CINNAMON PIE SCROLLS

MAKES 30 SCROLLS

½ batch Double Butter Crust dough (page 20)

Egg Wash (page 43)

⅓ cup (66 g) Cinnamon Sugar (page 254)

1. Prepare the dough (or collect the dough scraps) and chill in the fridge until you're ready to use it. If your dough is frozen, fully thaw it first.

2. Sprinkle your work surface with flour and use a rolling pin to start rolling the dough into a rectangular shape. If the disk is not getting larger as you roll, there's a good chance the dough is stuck to the surface below. Carefully lift the dough and add more flour to the surface. Continue rolling out the dough until you have a rectangle that is 8 by 12 inches and about ⅛ inch thick. The length will depend on how much dough you started with. Trim the edges, leaving a nice large rectangle.

3. Brush the whole surface of the dough with egg wash and sprinkle heavily with cinnamon sugar. The amount varies depending on how much delicious cinnamon sugar you want to add. I say go pretty heavy.

4. Starting on the short side, roll the dough tightly until you reach the middle. Repeat on the other side until it meets the middle. The end result will look like 2 connected scrolls. Chill in the freezer for at least 20 minutes.

5. Preheat the oven to 350°F. Line a baking sheet with parchment paper.

6. Use a sharp knife to carefully cut the chilled logs into ¼-inch-thick medallions. Place the medallions ½ inch apart on the prepared baking sheet. *Tip: If you aren't baking right away, wrap tightly with plastic wrap and freeze for up to 3 months. Thaw for 10 minutes before moving on to the next step.* Gently brush the surface of each medallion with the egg wash.

7. Bake for 15 to 20 minutes, until golden brown. Let cool completely. These can be stored in an airtight container for up to 4 days.

ie twists are as simple as roll, sprinkle, twist, and bake. And this recipe allows you to be as creative as you want. The two twists that we often make in the bakery are cheesy bacon twists and cheesy herb twists. While we go savory with our choices, you can certainly go the sweet route with cinnamon sugar, Nutella, toffee bits, or chopped-up fruit. The recipes below are guidelines only—if you really love a topping, feel free to add a little more. Can you ever have too much cheese?

PIE TWISTS

MAKES TWELVE 8-INCH TWISTS

½ batch Double Butter Crust dough (page 20)

⅓ cup (80 mL) melted butter

Toppings of your choice (see below)

Cheesy Bacon Topping

½ cup (227 g) crumbled cooked bacon

¾ cup (75 g) grated smoked cheddar cheese

Cheesy Herb Topping

⅓ cup (42 g) grated parmesan cheese

2 Tbsp chopped fresh herbs

Pinch sea salt

Cinnamon Sugar Topping

¼ cup (50 g) Cinnamon Sugar (page 254)

Nutella Topping

⅔ cup (197 g) Nutella

⅓ cup (50 g) finely chopped hazelnuts

1. Prepare the dough (or collect the dough scraps) and chill in the fridge until you're ready to use it. If your dough is frozen, fully thaw it first. Preheat the oven to 350°F. Line a baking sheet with parchment paper.

2. Sprinkle your work surface with flour, and use a rolling pin to roll out the dough. If the circumference is not getting larger as you roll, there's a good chance the dough is stuck to the surface below. Carefully lift the dough and add more flour to the surface. Continue rolling out the dough until it is about 12 by 16 inches wide and ⅛ inch thick.

3. Brush half the sheet of dough with butter. Sprinkle the desired toppings over the butter. Fold the other half of the dough over the toppings and use a rolling pin to give it a good roll to really seal in all the goodness.

4. Cut the sheet into strips about 1 inch wide and 8 to 10 inches long. Gently twist the strip 2 or 3 times and place on the prepared baking sheet. Brush the surface with even more butter.

5. Bake for 20 to 25 minutes, until golden brown. Remove from the oven and let cool completely.

note These will last for 3 days in an airtight container at room temperature or in the fridge, depending on the filling you choose. Just make sure to bring back to room temperature before serving.

f course we need to have a pie hole recipe, after all it is the name of my company! They are fun, they are flaky, and they are definitely for those who love pie crust. Then add a stick, and boom! You have a pie pop! Fruit—especially fruit compote—makes the best filling for these as the compote has already been reduced and thickened, which helps keep the filling inside.

PIE HOLES & PIE POPS

MAKES ABOUT 12 PIE HOLES OR POPS (PIE HOLES WITH STICKS!)

½ batch Double Butter Crust dough (page 20)

Egg Wash (page 43)

¼ cup (60 mL) fruit filling of your choice (page 262)

Sugar or Cinnamon Sugar (page 254), to coat

> **note** You can freeze the unbaked pie pops on the baking sheet, and, once frozen, place them in an airtight container and freeze for up to 3 months. When ready, bake them for 25 minutes right out of the freezer, as thawing will make them soggy.

1. Prepare the dough (or collect the dough scraps) and chill in the fridge until you're ready to use it. If your dough is frozen, fully thaw it first. Line a baking sheet with parchment paper. Preheat the oven to 350°F.

2. Sprinkle your work surface with flour and use a rolling pin to roll out the dough. If the circumference is not getting larger as you roll, there's a good chance the dough is stuck to the surface below. Carefully lift the dough and add more flour to the surface. Continue rolling out the dough until it is about ⅛ inch thick.

3. Use a 2-inch to 2½-inch circle cookie cutter to cut out 24 rounds of dough. Place 12 of the rounds 1 inch apart on the prepared baking sheet. Brush the whole surface of each round with egg wash.

4. To make a pie pop, gently press a wooden dowel into the center of 12 rounds, like a lollipop, so the top of the dowel is ¼ inch away from the opposite side of the round. If you're making pie holes, you don't need a stick. Dollop the filling in the center of each. Repeat for each round.

5. Cover each round with 1 of the remaining 12 rounds and use the back of a fork or your fingers to secure the top edges around the bottoms. Brush the tops with egg wash and sprinkle with sugar or cinnamon sugar. Cut a little "x" in the center to vent the pop.

6. Bake for 12 to 15 minutes until golden brown. Remove, cool completely, and eat!

ver the years, I have proclaimed that anything can go into a pie shell. This is an invitation for people to share their most absurd ingredient ideas with me. One of the most frequently suggested ideas was a poutine pie. Challenge accepted! Poutine is an iconic Canadian dish typically made with salty French fries with hot gravy poured over squeaky cheese curds. I wanted to make something that played with the idea, but with a twist, so I created this dessert poutine.

PIE POUTINE SUNDAE WITH PIE FRIES

MAKES 1 LARGE SUNDAE

Maple Buttercream "Curds"

½ cup (120 g) Maple Buttercream Frosting (page 270)

Pie Fries

½ batch Double Butter Crust dough (page 20)

Egg Wash (page 43)

Maple Caramel "Gravy"

1–3 scoops vanilla ice cream

¼ batch Maple Caramel Sauce (page 261)

note The pie fries are also great on their own with a little Caramel Sauce (page 258) or Lemon Meringue Pie filling (page 217) for dipping. Yum!

1. For the "curds," line a baking sheet with parchment paper. While the maple buttercream frosting is still nice and fluffy, spread it over the prepared baking sheet until it is about ¼ to ½ inch thick. Chill the buttercream for at least 20 minutes in the freezer, until frozen.

2. Break the chilled buttercream into little cheese curd–sized pieces. Store in an airtight container in the freezer for up to 3 months until ready to use.

3. For the pie fries, prepare the dough (or collect the dough scraps) and chill in the fridge. If your dough is frozen, fully thaw it first. Preheat the oven to 350°F. Line a baking sheet with parchment paper.

4. Sprinkle your work surface with flour and use a rolling pin to begin to roll out the dough. If the circumference is not getting larger as you roll, there's a good chance the dough is stuck to the surface below. Carefully lift the dough and add more flour to the surface. Continue rolling out the dough until the sheet of dough is about ⅛ inch thick. Cut into thin strips (roughly ¼ inch wide and 5 to 7 inches long) that resemble fries. They can vary in size just as fries do. Place the strips ½ inch apart on the prepared baking sheet. Brush the whole surface of each strip with egg wash.

5. Bake for 15 minutes until golden brown. Set aside to cool.

6. For the "gravy," in a sundae serving bowl (bigger is always better!), add some vanilla ice cream. Place the pie fries haphazardly over the ice cream. Top with a few tablespoons of the maple buttercream "curds" and pour warmed maple caramel sauce overtop. Be generous—it's delicious!

These are my favorite thing to make with extra dough, and they are the perfect little rustic dessert to serve guests. Yes, I would say I like serving them even more than pie . . . shhhhh! Warm from the oven with a big scoop of vanilla ice cream in the middle, these will seriously bring a smile to anyone's face. And it's a great way to use up any extra dough and fruit you have. You can use any of the fruit pie fillings to make galettes. You'll need about ½ cup of filling for each galette.

GALETTES

MAKES SIX 7-INCH GALETTES

1 batch Double Butter Crust dough (page 20)

3 cups fruit pie filling (we like the Bourbon Peach Crumble, page 126)

Egg Wash (page 43)

1 cup (150 g) Golden Sugar Pecan Crumble (page 251)

6 scoops vanilla ice cream (optional)

½ cup (125 mL) Caramel Sauce (page 258) (optional)

1. Prepare the dough (or collect the dough scraps) and chill in the fridge until you're ready to use it. If your dough is frozen, fully thaw it first. Preheat the oven to 350°F. Line a baking sheet with parchment paper.

2. Sprinkle your work surface with flour and use a rolling pin to start rolling half of the disk of dough. Rotate the dough 90 degrees after every few passes to work toward creating a circular shape. If the circumference of the disk is not getting larger as you roll, there's a good chance the dough is stuck to the surface below. Carefully lift the dough and add more flour to the surface. Continue rolling until the dough is about ⅛ inch thick.

3. Cut out six 7-inch rounds and place them on the prepared baking sheet. Evenly divide the fruit filling between the 6 galettes, placing the filling in the center. Fold the edges over to cover some of the filling. Remember, these are meant to look rustic. Brush the top of the folded pie crust with egg wash. Top the exposed filling with the golden sugar pecan crumble.

4. Bake for 35 to 40 minutes, until the juices are bubbling out and appear sticky. Let cool a little and serve warm with a generous scoop of ice cream. If you are feeling indulgent, drizzle with some caramel sauce.

opping a pie with a crumble has a few important and delicious reasons. The most important is that the crumble acts as a barrier to protect the fruit from burning during the baking. A crumble also provides a beautiful buttery textural contrast to the flaky pastry below and can be a wonderful way to impart different flavors. It is also a great base for flavor-amplifying ingredients like nuts, cinnamon, zests, and coconut. At The Pie Hole, I choose between a Golden Sugar Crumble (page 250) and a White Sugar Crumble (page 251) based on the recipe.

Pie connoisseurs are often split between full-top-crust fans and crumble-top fans. At The Pie Hole, we like to provide a variety so there is something for everyone. Adding a golden sugar crumble to any fruit pie is like putting a cozy little sweater on it. Pro tip: hiding a nice drizzle of caramel on top of the fruit filling, before you sprinkle on the crumble, makes for pure heaven.

GOLDEN SUGAR CRUMBLE

MAKES ENOUGH CRUMBLE FOR ONE 9-INCH PIE

½ cup (114 g) butter, cold

1 cup (150 g) flour

½ cup (100 g) golden sugar

note You can use brown sugar instead of golden sugar. I just happen to prefer the taste of golden sugar.

1. Cut the butter into 1-inch pieces.

2. Using a stand mixer fitted with the paddle attachment, combine the flour and sugar for 30 seconds on the lowest setting until mixed. Add the cold butter, a few pieces at a time, mixing until you have a coarse, crumbly texture that holds together when squeezed. Do not overmix, or you will start to cream the butter, and you will lose that beautiful crumbly texture.

Variations

GOLDEN SUGAR PRALINE CRUMBLE

As above plus:

½ cup (60 g) coarsely chopped pecans

¼ cup (40 g) rolled oats

note This crumble would be a delicious substitution on the Apple Buttermilk Crumble (page 104), Apple Caramel Crumble (page 111), or Cherry Pie (page 134) with a crumble top instead of top crust.

In step 2, as the crumble is beginning to come together, add the pecans and rolled oats and continue to mix for an additional 30 to 45 seconds in the stand mixer until fully combined.

GOLDEN SUGAR PECAN CRUMBLE

As on page 250 plus:

½ tsp cinnamon

½ cup (60 g) coarsely chopped
   pecans

In step 2, add the cinnamon, and then, as the crumble is beginning to come together, add the pecans and continue to mix for an additional 30 seconds in the stand mixer until fully combined.

BACON GOLDEN SUGAR CRUMBLE

As on page 250 plus:

6 slices cooked bacon, crumbled

In step 2, as the crumble is beginning to come together, add the bacon and continue to mix for an additional 30 to 45 seconds in the stand mixer until fully combined.

As a general rule of thumb, I believe that pies that are spiced with cinnamon and nutmeg are cozy and need that golden sugar love, while berry pies are fresh and bright, and that is where the white sugar crumble really shines. These are just my feelings, so please feel free to interchange the crumbles. Add some golden sugar crumble to a pie that needs a little hug.

WHITE SUGAR CRUMBLE

**MAKES ENOUGH CRUMBLE
FOR ONE 9-INCH PIE**

1 cup (227 g) butter, cold

1½ cups (225 g) flour

1 cup (200 g) sugar

1. Cut the butter into 1-inch pieces.

2. Using a stand mixer fitted with the paddle attachment, combine the flour and sugar for 30 seconds on the lowest setting until mixed. Add the cold butter, a few pieces at a time, mixing until you have a coarse, crumbly texture that holds together when squeezed. Do not overmix, or you will start to cream the butter, and you will lose that beautiful crumbly texture.

WHITE SUGAR CINNAMON CRUMBLE

As on page 251 plus:

½ tsp of cinnamon

In step 2, add the cinnamon. This is a nice topping for the Apple Buttermilk Crumble (page 104).

WHITE SUGAR COCONUT CRUMBLE

As on page 251 plus:

¼ cup (25 g) unsweetened shredded coconut

In step 2, as the crumble is beginning to come together, add the coconut and continue to mix for an additional 30 to 45 seconds in the stand mixer.

WHITE SUGAR ALMOND CRUMBLE

As on page 251 plus:

⅓ cup (45 g) slivered almonds

In step 2, as the crumble is beginning to come together, add the almonds and continue to mix for an additional 30 seconds. This is a divine twist when added to the top of the Blueberry Goat Cheese Basil Pie (page 122).

WHITE SUGAR CITRUS CRUMBLE

As on page 251 plus:

1 Tbsp citrus zest (lemon, lime, or orange)

Before step 2, add the citrus zest into the sugar and mix well. Add to the flour and follow the rest of the instructions. Lemon zest is the perfect accompaniment to our Blueberry Pie (page 121), lime zest elevates our Raspberry Cream Crumble (page 133).

> **note** You can make your crumble up to 3 days in advance. Just keep it in an airtight container in the refrigerator. Much like pie dough, the crumble should be cold when it goes into the oven to help retain the shape and texture.

I love, love, love banana bread. It was the first and only thing I learned to bake with my Nan Parsons. I baked banana bread with her to bring to my new baby sister at the hospital the day she was born (don't worry, the nurses ate it). Years later, I also brought banana bread and pie for the nurses when my own daughter was born—I didn't realize it was a tradition until now. While you don't need to top your To Die for Banana Cream Pie (page 171) with banana bread crumble, it is how we do it at The Pie Hole.

BANANA BREAD CRUMBLE

MAKES 1 LOAF OR ENOUGH CRUMBLE FOR ONE 9-INCH PIE

2 eggs, beaten

⅓ cup (80 mL) buttermilk

½ cup (125 mL) vegetable oil

1 tsp vanilla

1 cup mashed bananas (about 3 bananas)

1½ cups (300 g) sugar

1¾ cups (263 g) flour

1 tsp baking soda

1 tsp cinnamon

½ tsp salt

½ cup (100 g) chocolate chunks

note If you don't have buttermilk, just add 1 tsp of lemon juice to regular milk and let it stand until it curdles (about 5 minutes).

1. Preheat the oven to 325°F. Grease and flour a loaf pan or spray with a nonstick cooking spray or line with parchment paper.

2. In a large bowl, combine the beaten eggs, buttermilk, oil, vanilla, and mashed bananas.

3. In a medium bowl, sift the sugar, flour, baking soda, cinnamon, and salt.

4. Add the dry ingredients to the wet ingredients and combine, mixing well to fully incorporate. Gently fold half the chocolate into the batter. Transfer to the prepared loaf pan.

5. Bake for 60 minutes, add the remaining chocolate chunks on top and continue to bake for another 10 to 20 minutes, until a wooden skewer comes out clean. Let cool completely.

6. Crumble as needed for the topping of banana cream pie and have a few slices for yourself. Tightly wrap your cooled banana bread to keep it moist, and try to enjoy it all within 3 days, if it even lasts that long. You can always freeze a little in an airtight container (for up to 2 months) to have on hand for topping your banana cream pies.

I t doesn't get simpler than this recipe: just one ingredient, a baking sheet, and either a preheated oven or stovetop, and within minutes the heavenly aroma of toasted coconut comes wafting through the kitchen. It is almost magical how much toasting transforms coconut. The nuttiness comes out, and the texture becomes nice and crisp. Toasted coconut is not only a delicious snack on its own (I could easily eat a bowl of it), but also a wonderful topping on pies, cakes, cupcakes, and whipped cream–topped hot drinks.

TOASTED COCONUT

MAKES 2 CUPS

2 cups (226 g) unsweetened
    coconut, ribbons or shredded

1. Preheat the oven to 350°F and line a baking sheet with parchment paper, or set a large skillet over medium heat.

2. Spread the coconut in an even single layer on the prepared baking sheet and bake for 6 to 8 minutes, tossing at the halfway point. Alternatively, toast the coconut in the skillet for a few minutes, stirring constantly. When the coconut starts to brown, turn off the heat under the skillet but continue stirring to evenly brown the coconut with the residual heat of the pan.

3. Transfer to a plate and allow to cool. Toasted coconut will keep for 3 to 4 weeks in an airtight container.

A ll of our double-crust fruit pies get a full egg wash (page 43) to give them that beautiful brown color when baking. We also sprinkle sugar or cinnamon sugar on top depending on the recipe. My rule is that anything with apples in it gets cinnamon sugar for that added little cinnamon taste. While you certainly do not have to do this step, I love the way it looks when it bakes and the way it tastes when I am stuffing my pie hole. Also, it doesn't get easier than this recipe.

CINNAMON SUGAR

MAKES ABOUT 1 CUP

1 cup (200 g) white sugar

2 Tbsp ground cinnamon

1. In a small bowl, mix the sugar and the cinnamon until evenly combined.

2. Store in an airtight container until ready to sprinkle.

A little play on the idea of magical fairy dust. Berries and summer fruits are awfully juicy, and that is what makes them so delicious. It also makes them harder to work with when making a pie. All the extra juice can cause soggy-bottom pies, and no one wants a soggy bottom. We add a thin coating of "B"airy Dust to the bottom of our juiciest pies (like Blueberry Pie (page 121), Strawberry Rhubarb Pie (page 138), Cherry Pie (page 134), or Juicy Peach Pie (page 129) to help thicken and absorb some of the juice. It's super easy to make, and you can just store it in a jar all summer. It will come in handy for all the pie making you will be doing.

"B"AIRY DUST

MAKES 2 CUPS

1 cup (150 g) flour
1 cup (200 g) sugar

1. In a medium mixing bowl, whisk the flour and the sugar together.

2. Transfer to an airtight container and keep on hand for all your juicy pie-making days. This mixture can last almost forever, so it is nice to make it ahead and have it on hand.

3. Once you have your pie docked and ready for the fruit filling, sprinkle 2 to 3 Tbsp over the bottom of the crust. Top with fruit and finish the pie with a full top, lattice, or crumble.

There are a lot of pies that come out of the oven ready to impress. A perfectly oozy gooey apple pie or a lattice-topped strawberry rhubarb pie are sure to make you swoon. But some pies require a little extra love post-baking to elevate them to drool-worthy status. Adding a little something to the top of a pie, slice, pop tart, or sundae is how we roll.

Pour some Sugar on me

little bourbon can be such a nice complement to pies. So we make an icing glaze spiked with bourbon. It is up to you how much you want to drizzle on top. I like to put on a lot . . . party on!

BOURBON DRIZZLE

MAKES ¼ CUP

½ cup (70 g) icing sugar

2 tsp milk

2 tsp bourbon

1. In a small bowl, combine the icing sugar, milk, and bourbon and mix until smooth.

2. Drizzle over a chilled pie. Store the remaining bourbon drizzle in an airtight container in the fridge for up to 2 weeks.

h good lord, who doesn't want to drizzle caramel over everything? I post pictures on our social media and people go crazy seeing all of that caramel pouring down over the ice cream pie topping. We make all of our caramel in-house and in huge pots as we use so much of it every day! A few simple ingredients and you have a pot of caramel. Make extra as it keeps really well in an airtight container.

CARAMEL SAUCE

MAKES 2 CUPS

1½ cups (300 g) sugar

½ cup (125 mL) water

2 Tbsp butter

1 cup (250 mL) heavy cream

1 tsp vanilla

1. In a medium saucepan, add the sugar and water. Heat over high heat, without stirring, until the sugar dissolves completely. Allow the mixture to boil for 7 to 10 minutes, or until it turns a beautiful rich caramel color.

2. Once the sauce is a rich caramel color, remove from the heat and quickly add the butter. It will melt fast. Slowly pour in the cream (the caramel will bubble up) and stir until it is all combined. Mix in the vanilla.

3. Let the sauce cool to room temperature and then transfer to an airtight container. Store your caramel sauce in the refrigerator for up to 2 weeks. If there is any separation in the sauce, just give it a quick stir before using it.

came up with this insanely good caramel sauce variation specifically to top our dessert poutine in the days leading up to Canada Day.

MAPLE CARAMEL SAUCE

MAKES 2¾ CUPS

2¼ cups (560 mL) pure maple syrup

1 cup (250 mL) heavy cream

¼ cup (60 mL) corn syrup

¼ cup (57 g) butter

1 tsp sea salt flakes

1 tsp vanilla

note Store in an airtight container in the fridge for up to 2 weeks.

1. In a large saucepan over medium-high heat, bring the maple syrup to a boil. Do not stir. Heat the mixture until a candy thermometer or temperature gun measures 215°F, 10 to 12 minutes. It will bubble up a lot, so keep an eye on it.

2. Meanwhile, in a medium saucepan over medium heat, combine the cream, corn syrup, butter, salt, and vanilla. Bring to a low simmer, stirring frequently.

3. Once the maple syrup has reached the desired temperature, remove it from the heat. Very slowly add the hot cream mixture. The maple syrup is extremely hot and will bubble up with the addition of the cream. Stir until the syrup stops bubbling and sounding like a witch's potion and is fully combined.

4. Return the combined mixture to the stovetop over medium heat. Bring it back to a simmer, stirring constantly, and cook for an additional 1 to 2 minutes. Remove from the heat and let cool at room temperature for a couple of hours.

t's pretty handy to have a squeezey bottle of chocolate ganache kicking around. It's so simple to make, with just two ingredients, and you can vary the ratio to get different consistencies. For drizzling, a 1:1 ratio works perfectly.

CHOCOLATE GANACHE

MAKES 1⅔ CUPS

¾ cup (130 g) semi-sweet chocolate chips

½ cup (125 mL) heavy cream

note Store in an airtight container in the fridge for up to 3 weeks or the freezer for up to 3 months

1. Place the chocolate chips in a large heatproof bowl.

2. Heat the cream in a small saucepan over medium heat until it just starts to boil, then carefully pour over the chocolate chips. Let sit for 3 minutes for the cream to begin to melt the chocolate.

3. Slowly whisk together to incorporate the cream and chocolate, keeping the whisk in the center of the bowl to start, so the hot cream does not splash out.

4. If drizzling over whipped cream, let the ganache cool for 10 to 15 minutes first. For a nice fluffy whipped ganache frosting, whip the completely cooled ganache in a stand mixer fitted with the whisk attachment.

F ruit compote is the best topping for a sundae. My favorite is Strawberry Rhubarb, an iconic pie flavor that's a little sweet, a little tart. And I had to include this Sour Cherry Compote, not only because we put it on top of our Black Forest Pie (page 203) and the Vegan Chocolate Hazelnut Pie (page 167), but also because one of my closest friends, now lovingly known as Uncle Mo, will literally eat it by the bowlful. If it were up to him, he would have cherry compote on everything.

FRUIT COMPOTE

MAKES 2 CUPS

Strawberry Rhubarb Compote

1 cup sliced fresh strawberries

1 cup diced rhubarb, ½-inch pieces

¼ cup (50 g) sugar

2 Tbsp water

1 Tbsp cornstarch

1 tsp lemon juice

1 tsp vanilla

Peach Compote

2½ cups sliced fresh peaches

½ cup (100 g) sugar

⅓ cup (80 mL) water

¼ tsp cinnamon

1 Tbsp cornstarch

1 Tbsp lemon juice

1 Tbsp vanilla

Sour Cherry Compote

2½ cups frozen sour cherries, pitted

½ cup (100 g) sugar

1 Tbsp water

1 Tbsp cornstarch

2 tsp lemon juice

½ tsp bitters

Blueberry Compote

2 cups blueberries, fresh or frozen

⅓ cup (66 g) sugar

3 Tbsp water

2 tsp cornstarch

1 Tbsp lemon juice

Raspberry Compote

4 cups raspberries, fresh or frozen

¼ cup (50 g) sugar

¼ cup (60 mL) water

1 Tbsp cornstarch

2 Tbsp lemon juice

note To make a vegan version of this compote, use organic cane sugar.

1. In a medium saucepan over medium heat, combine the fruit, sugar, water, and cinnamon if included, and cook, stirring frequently, until the fruit starts to break down. For Sour Cherry, if you are using fresh sour cherries you can omit the water.

2. Meanwhile, in a small bowl, combine the cornstarch, lemon juice, and vanilla (if included) and mix until smooth.

3. Using a spatula, add the lemon mixture to the fruit mixture. Stirring constantly, bring to a boil and cook until thickened and the fruit is tender. Remove from heat and let cool completely before using.

4. Store in an airtight container in the fridge for up to 2 weeks.

y husband might love whipped cream more than anyone I have ever met. When he was growing up, his mom would make him and his brothers fresh whipped cream to eat by the bowlful. How he has stayed skinny I will never know. To this day, I have to keep an eye on him when I'm making whipped cream. Even his pie-to-whipped-cream ratio is way off (or right on, depending where you stand), but I get it, whipped cream is a wonderful pairing for pie.

WHIPPED CREAM

MAKES 3½ CUPS

2 cups (500 mL) heavy cream

2 Tbsp icing sugar

1 packet whipped cream stabilizer (optional) (see Note)

1 tsp vanilla (optional) (see Note)

1. In the bowl of your stand mixer fitted with the whisk attachment, combine the cream, icing sugar, whipped cream stabilizer, and vanilla over medium speed until stiff peaks form.

2. You can use either a spoon or a piping bag to top your pie with whipped cream.

note The whipped cream stabilizer is optional, but unless you plan to make and finish the pie the same day, it will help keep the whipped cream from falling flat. It can usually be found in little packages in the baking aisle at your grocery store. The vanilla is also optional, but if you have it, use it because it really elevates the whipped cream.

Variations

PEANUT BUTTER WHIPPED CREAM

Add: ⅓ cup (85 g) smooth creamy peanut butter

Once the cream has reached a medium-firm peak, add the peanut butter and continue to mix until a stiff peak is reached. Do not use chunky peanut butter if you intend to pipe the cream, as it will just block your piping tip and become very messy.

CARAMEL WHIPPED CREAM

Add: ¼ cup (60 mL) Caramel Sauce (page 258).

Once the cream has reached a medium-firm peak, add the caramel sauce. Continue to whisk until firm peaks form.

VANILLA BEAN WHIPPED CREAM

Add: Whole or half vanilla bean pod cut lengthwise, seeds scraped

Either replace the vanilla extract with scraped seeds from a whole or half vanilla bean pod or use half the bean pod and 1 tsp of pure vanilla extract to intensify the flavor. It just depends on how much delicious vanilla flavor you want.

ESPRESSO COFFEE WHIPPED CREAM

Add: 2 oz shot espresso

Once you have reached a medium-firm peak, add the espresso. Continue to whisk until firm peaks form.

KIRSCH WHIPPED CREAM

Add: 1 oz kirsch (cherry-flavored liqueur)

Once you have reached a medium-firm peak, add the kirsch. Continue to whisk until firm peaks are achieved. This goes really great on top of the Black Forest Pie (page 203).

D o you love whipped cream and chocolate? If so, this might just be the best thing ever! This is easy to make and goes really well on a few different pies. We use it as a whole layer on our Triple Chocolate Cream Pie (page 189), and it also goes really well with the Peanut Butter Cup Pie (page 163).

CHOCOLATE WHIPPED CREAM

MAKES 4 CUPS

½ cup (85 g) semi-sweet chocolate chips

2 cups (500 mL) heavy cream

1 Tbsp cocoa powder

1 Tbsp icing sugar

1. Place the chocolate chips in a large heat-proof bowl and set aside.

2. In a small saucepan over medium-high heat, whisk 1 cup of the cream and the cocoa powder. Once it starts to boil, remove immediately and pour over the chocolate chips. Let sit for 3 minutes. The heat from the cream will begin to melt the chocolate. Then slowly start to whisk, starting in the middle and working your way to the outer edges to keep the hot cream from splashing out. Continue whisking until the mixture is very smooth.

3. Add the remaining cream and icing sugar, and stir to fully incorporate. Chill for 1 hour minimum. The colder the better.

4. Using a stand mixer fitted with the whisk attachment, whip the cooled chocolate mixture until stiff peaks form.

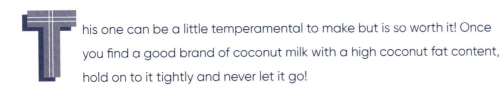

This one can be a little temperamental to make but is so worth it! Once you find a good brand of coconut milk with a high coconut fat content, hold on to it tightly and never let it go!

VEGAN COCONUT WHIP

MAKES 2 CUPS

Coconut fat from 1 sealed can (14 oz/398 mL) coconut cream or milk

¼ cup (35 g) organic icing sugar

1 Tbsp maple syrup

1. Chill the sealed can of coconut milk overnight, along with your mixing bowl and beaters.

2. When you're ready to make the coconut whip, flip the can over, open the bottom, and drain the fluid. Whip the coconut fat until smooth, then add the icing sugar and maple syrup. Mix until incorporated.

3. Use immediately or keep in the fridge for up to 2 weeks in an airtight container.

To make the most decadent chocolaty bite of heaven for Valentine's Day, my head chef suggested that we top our Triple Chocolate Cream Pie (page 189) with a whipped white chocolate ganache. This is why I love her . . . and it was delicious and to die for! And this is coming from someone who unapologetically pronounces a love for vanilla when asked to pick sides. I find myself, however, trying to find reasons to add this topping to every pie.

WHIPPED WHITE CHOCOLATE GANACHE

MAKES 5 CUPS

2⅔ cups (660 mL) heavy cream, cold

1 Tbsp glucose syrup

1½ cups (255 g) white chocolate chips (we use Callebaut)

1. In a medium saucepan over medium heat, combine 1 cup of the cream and the glucose and bring to a simmer. Do not boil.

2. Carefully add the white chocolate to the hot cream and glucose mixture and let sit for 2 minutes.

3. Slowly start to whisk, starting in the middle then working your way to the outer edges to keep the hot cream from splashing out. Continue whisking until the mixture is very smooth.

4. Let cool to room temperature. Once cooled, add the remaining cream and whisk in until combined. Chill in an airtight container for 24 hours.

5. Using a stand mixer fitted with the whisk attachment or a hand mixer in a larger bowl, whip the white chocolate ganache until stiff peaks form. Use right away.

t's soft and billowy, and oh so perfect for topping a pie. We top a few different pies with this. The most obvious would be Lemon Meringue Pie (page 217), but we also use this heavenly cloud-like topping on our Butterscotch Pie (page 191), Pink Lemonade Pie (page 214), and S'more Pie (page 207).

ITALIAN MERINGUE

MAKES ENOUGH FOR ONE 9-INCH PIE

1 cup (200 g) sugar

⅓ cup (80 mL) water

4 egg whites

> **note** It is very important to use a very clean bowl for the egg whites that is free of any oil or fat. You can quickly wipe the bowl with paper towel lightly dampened with white vinegar.

1. In a small saucepan, combine the sugar and the water and set over medium-high heat. Do not stir. Let the mixture simmer until a candy thermometer or temperature gun measures 250°F, 5 to 7 minutes.

2. Meanwhile, place the egg whites in the bowl of a stand mixer fitted with the whisk attachment. When the sugar mixture reaches 230°F, you can start to whip the egg whites on medium speed.

3. Once the desired temperature is reached and your egg whites form soft peaks, drop the mixer speed to low. Very slowly add the hot sugar mixture in a steady stream to the bowl of the stand mixer. Try not to pour the syrup into the whisk, as that could result in hot sugar flying out at you! When all of the syrup has been added, bring the speed up to medium-high and whip until stiff peaks form and the bowl is cooler to the touch. The meringue should have a beautiful glossy sheen to it.

4. Use a spoon or a piping bag to spread the meringue immediately over a cooled pie. Use a kitchen torch to carefully brown the meringue, or place the pie on a parchment-lined baking sheet on the bottom rack of your oven and broil for 3 to 4 minutes. Caution: Meringue can burn quickly, so keep the top of the pie at least 6 inches from the broiler and keep your eyes on it. A watched meringue never burns!

Variations

PRETTY IN PINK MERINGUE

Add: 2 or 3 drops light pink food coloring or 1 or 2 drops red food coloring

In step 3, after the sugar mixture has been added and just before you turn the speed back up, add the food coloring. Gel food coloring works best, as it is very concentrated and doesn't add much fluid. Continue to mix according to the recipe.

LAVENDER MERINGUE

Add: 1 Tbsp dried lavender buds

In step 1, add the lavender buds to the sugar and water to infuse the lavender flavor. Once the mixture has reached temperature, use a small sieve to quickly strain the syrup to remove the lavender. Continue on with the rest of the meringue recipe. This is so lovely on our Earl Grey Cream Pie (page 177) in place of the whipped cream.

ORANGE BOURBON MERINGUE

Add: 1 Tbsp fresh orange zest

1 Tbsp bourbon

In step 1, add the orange zest to the sugar and water to infuse the orange flavor. Add the bourbon after the hot sugar mixture and continue to whip until stiff peaks form.

his is a very fluffy, delicious, and easy-to make buttercream that I also use for all my daughter's birthday cakes. Yes, I do make cakes sometimes.

BUTTERCREAM FROSTING

MAKES 2¾ CUPS

1 cup (227 g) butter, at room temperature

2 cups (280 g) icing sugar

2 tsp vanilla extract

1. Using a stand mixer fitted with the paddle attachment over medium-high speed, beat the butter until it is light in color and very fluffy, 30 seconds to 1 minute. Scrape down the sides of the bowl as needed.

2. Stop the mixer. Add half of the icing sugar, then mix with the stand mixer running on low speed. Stop the mixer and add the second half of the icing sugar. Again, with the mixer running on low speed, mix until fully incorporated. Turn the speed to medium-high and beat the mixture for 2 to 3 minutes until light and fluffy.

3. Add the vanilla and mix until incorporated. Store in the fridge for up to 1 week.

Variations

MAPLE BUTTERCREAM FROSTING

As above but substitute vanilla for:

2 tsp maple extract

In step 3, replace the vanilla with the maple extract.

MULTICOLORED BUTTERCREAM FROSTING

1 drop food coloring of your choice

In step 3, after the vanilla, add the food coloring. Or if you are looking for 2 different colors, split the frosting into 2 batches and hand stir the desired color into each batch. Our Birthday Cake Pie (page 198) uses 1 drop of the Regal Purple from Americolor gel food coloring.

Thank-Yous

I believe there is something very nostalgic about pies; they can evoke a lot of memories through look, taste, and smell. Each bite of pie my customers take is like a buttery hug from me. I have truly given my whole heart to creating these recipes, and each of the shops is an extension of my own personal style. I wouldn't be where I am at today without some very important people who have supported me this entire journey.

Thank you to my loving husband, Marlon. You have been there since day 1. You have graciously given me so much love and support. From packing and setting up my tent at the farmers' markets to building me three shops, it sure has been a ride! You are the original dough boy—I bet you never thought you would become so good at rolling dough! I seriously could not have asked for a better partner in life. I cannot thank you enough.

Thank you to my daughter, Cali. You may be only five years old but you have taught me so much already. I am a better person for being your momma. The Pie Hole wouldn't have survived if you were not such an amazing and patient baby. You spent your first 18 months of life working full time in the bakery, getting paid next to nothing. I promised you $1/day and I never paid you. Eighteen years from now with interest that is really going to cost me.

Thank you to my amazing sister, Carla. When you were living in New Zealand and would call me to talk about pie and dream up big plans, did you even think The Pie Hole would get to where it is today? I certainly didn't. Anytime I need you, I know you will be there right by my side. You are my best friend and I love you to pieces.

Thank you to my parents, Toni and Carl. I already dedicated this book to my mom, my biggest advocate, and I want to thank my Dad, the hardest working man I know. He worked his whole life to give us everything. He instilled in me the strong work ethic that I have today, and that I hope I pass down to my daughter. He taught me patience, compassion and to keep things copasetic. Love you, dad.

Thank you Christopher Kape. Your immense contribution to not only the growth of The Pie Hole but also to me is invaluable. You have provided me with so much guidance, encouragement, and wisdom as we navigate through the world of pie and business together. You have been so patient in putting up with all my crazy antics. Also, to Stacy Kape our cheerleader. No one looks better in a Pie Hole shirt.

Thank you to my dear friend, Morris. You are not only my chief taster but also a shoulder to lean on. You have provided honest feedback and helped me grow. You are one of the most patient and dependable people I have ever met, which is why I have trusted you with the most important thing in my life: Cali.

Thank you to my best friends, Melissa and Kelsey. You have both been there to roll up your sleeves and make pies anytime I have asked. I love you both and there are no other people I would rather drink bubbles with (of course with Carla too).

Thank you to Brian Way. I know I can call you any time of the day and you will be there for me. You are such an important part of our family and I am so happy my sister has such an amazing partner. You are a brother to me.

Thank you to Erin Sousa. You have made sure to make not only our pies look as beautiful as possible but also me, and I need someone to keep me together most days. Your hard work has made The Pie Hole a more recognizable brand. Thank you for being a confidante and someone I can truly trust. I would be remiss not to also thank your husband, Roberto. Always squeezing me in last minute to make me look good for all the photoshoots.

Thank you Janis Nicolay, my photographer for this book. Your talent amazes me and is clearly seen oozing from the pages of this book and many others you have worked on. I am going to miss shooting with you, forcing you to stuff your pie hole, and your playful sense of humour.

Thank you to the Appetite team. You guys took a chance to let me write a book. To share a piece of my journey, my stories, my successes, and my recipes. You have shown me so much patience as I wrote my first book.

Thank you to my staff, past and present. You have all played an important part in this story. You have taught me to trust. I always believed that to do something right you have to do it yourself, but there comes a point where you cannot do it all, and I have been so lucky to have so many people have my back. You are all family to me.

Thank you Erv and Carey Salvador. You both have supported and encouraged me. You gave me the opportunity to turn my pie-making hobby into a business through your generosity.

Thank you to friends, family, neighbors and the community: Christopher Mauro, Jess Elton, Darren St. Laurent, Matt Way, George Vinson, Dave Vinson, Deborah Dunne, Lynda Moss, Windsor Plywood Vancouver, Thane and Kirsten Pipes, Garden Party Flowers, Allan Hughes, East Van Roasters, Emily Upham, our loyal customers, Josh Boettcher, Futurpreneur, Annika Reinhardt, Jerry Wong, Everd Quiamco, Jamie Myers, Paul Bircham, Brett Isfeld, and fablehome.co.

Index